Advance Praise for
My Life of Dialogue.
Engaging Buddhists and Muslims

"On November 10, 2017, in Taiwan, my predecessor, Jean-Louis Cardinal Tauran, presented Donald Mitchell with a Certificate of Appreciation for his 30 years of 'outstanding contributions and tireless effort to foster the Church's dialogue with Buddhism.' He also gifted him the Papal Medallion as a recognition of Mitchell's continuous engagement in Buddhist-Christian dialogue as well as his work in the area of the dialogue of fraternity especially Buddhist-Christian projects of fraternity with for homeless in the USA. In his book, *My Life of Dialogue*, Mitchell invites readers to enter into the dynamic and content of a dialogue of the heart whereby brothers and sisters of different religious traditions come together to more deeply unite the human family."

—His Eminence Cardinal Miguel Ángel Ayuso Guixot, MCCJ
President, Pontifical Council for Interreligious Dialogue

"In the 1960s—at the height of the Cold War, the intensification of the Vietnam War, and global anxiety over nuclear tests and the proliferation of nuclear warheads—religious people around the world rose up for the cause of peace. Vatican II was the start of a global coalition of religious leaders, one of whom was my grandfather, a Japanese Buddhist. *My Life of Dialogue* offers fresh perspective into this interreligious history. Donald Mitchell's moving personal journey of spiritual and dialogical evolution also serves as a practical guide for people everywhere who earnestly seek a kind of dialogue that is an indispensable prerequisite to humanity realizing a real, just, inclusive, and lasting peace on Earth."

—Rev. Kosho Niwano
President-designate, Rissho Kosei-kai

"Traditionally, interfaith engagement happens during conferences and forums with formal discussions. Donald Mitchell is one of the few persons who has the gift to engage in dialogue of the heart that connects persons as well as doctrines. His life in dialogue has brought forward love, mercy, compassion, and action that counter narratives of violent ideologies throughout the world. His book, *My Life of Dialogue*, presents his vision and choice to live a life of heartfelt dialogue that has touched so many lives around the world, including mine. His work in the Philippines contributed to the peace agreement on March 27, 2014 between the Philippine Government and the Moro Islamic Liberation Front."

—Dean Macrina Marados
Institute of Islamic Studies, University of the Philippines

My Life of Dialogue
Engaging Buddhists and Muslims

My Life of Dialogue
Engaging Buddhists and Muslims

DONALD W. MITCHELL

forewords by
HIS HOLINESS THE DALAI LAMA
HIS EMINENCE FRANCIS CARDINAL ARINZE
HIS REVEREND DR. SAYYID M. SYEED

A Herder & Herder Book
THE CROSSROAD PUBLISHING COMPANY
NEW YORK

A Herder & Herder Book
The Crossroad Publishing Company www.crossroadpublishing.com

© 2021 by Donald W. Mitchell

Crossroad, Herder & Herder, and the crossed C logo/colophon are registered trademarks of The Crossroad Publishing Company.

All rights reserved. No part of this book may be copied, scanned, reproduced in any way, or stored in a retrieval system, or transmitted, in any form or by any means, electronic, mechanical, photocopying, recording, or otherwise, without the written permission of The Crossroad Publishing Company. For permission please write to rights@crossroadpublishing.com.

In continuation of our 200-year tradition of independent publishing, The Crossroad Publishing Company proudly offers a variety of books with strong, original voices and diverse perspectives. The viewpoints expressed in our books are not necessarily those of The Crossroad Publishing Company, any of its imprints, or of its employees, executives, or owners. Although the author and publisher have made every effort to ensure that the information in this book was correct at press time, the author and publisher do not assume and hereby disclaim any liability to any party for any loss, damage, or disruption caused by errors or omissions, whether such errors or omissions result from negligence, accident, or any other cause. No claims are made or responsibility assumed for any health or other benefits.

The text of this book is set in 12/16 Sabon LT Pro.

Composition by Rachel Dlugos
Cover design by Sophie Appel

Library of Congress Cataloging-in-Publication Data
available upon request from the Library of Congress.

ISBN 978-0-8245-9701-6 paperback
ISBN 978-0-8245-0478-6 cloth
ISBN 978-0-8245-0480-9 ePub
ISBN 978-0-8245-0481-6 mobi

Books published by The Crossroad Publishing Company may be purchased at special quantity discount rates for classes and institutional use. For information, please e-mail sales@crossroadpublishing.com.

In Memoriam

Chiara Lubich
1920–2008

FOREWORD

THE DALAI LAMA

His Holiness the Dalai Lama

All our different religious traditions convey the message of love, compassion, tolerance, and contentment. As human beings, our lives begin in the shelter of our mothers' care and affection, without which we would not survive. It is our basic human nature to love and be loved. Different religious traditions uphold their different philosophical standpoints, but all are focused on love and compassion in practice.

A spirit of mutual admiration and respect among our religious traditions is extremely important. It will arise naturally if we engage in dialogue and educate one another in our different approaches.

I am happy to see that Donald W. Mitchell has documented his experience of interreligious discourse in this book, which recounts efforts to build interreligious harmony in action.

September 17, 2019
Dharamsala, India

FOREWORD

His Eminence Francis Cardinal Arinze

My *Life of Dialogue* is a beautiful presentation of the practical involvement of Professor Donald W. Mitchell in dialogues between Christians and Buddhists and Muslims. The reader will find in the two chapters about his work for our Pontifical Council for Interreligious Dialogue admirable examples of sharing between Christians and Buddhists, not just in matters academic but also, and especially, in actual heartfelt living and in the joint promotion of projects that benefit society. Dr. Mitchell has gone beyond just being a professor. He lives dialogue. He shows that it is possible for a convinced Christian to meet a convinced Buddhist, not just in mutual listening and discussion, but also in heartfelt sharing, mutual learning, and edification, helping to build unity.

Dr. Mitchell's continued cooperation with the Pontifical Council for Interreligious Dialogue for the past thirty-five years in ever-more-engaging dialogues with Buddhists and his other initiatives have helped for a better appreciation of what is distinctive of Christianity and of Buddhism. Mutual enrichment has been a result. Inter-monastic exchanges have been promoted. Deeper engagement in Christian–Buddhist dialogues has helped engender a more persevering pursuit of the truth and has been an important contribution to peacebuilding, to the dialogue of fraternity, to healing, to reconciliation, and to helping the poor and needy. Dr. Mitchell is to be congratulated because he is carrying out what the Second Vatican Council exhorted Christians to do, namely, that they should "through dialogue and collaboration, with the followers of other religions, and in witness of Christian faith and life, acknowledge, preserve, and promote the spiritual and moral goods found among these men, as well as the virtues in their society and culture" (*Nostra Aetate*, 2). It is deeply enriching to read *My Life of Dialogue*!

October 4, 2019
Vatican City

FOREWORD

His Reverend Dr. Sayyid M. Syeed

I would like to congratulate Professor Donald Mitchell for writing this powerful narrative of his global mission of peacebuilding. It is an inspiring account of an American man of religion going abroad, committed to exploring how to contribute to building peace in extremely dangerous regions. The question is, what inspired him and what made him tread where highly trained American persons equipped with the most lethal of weapons are not able to bring even a semblance of peace?

Catholics and Muslims, with similar global demographics, had fought holy wars for a millennium and continued to be suspicious and religiously mistrustful of each other. Then, Vatican II opened the door to building a new relationship between the two religions. Prophet Muhammad was no longer a false prophet inspired by Satan. *Nostra Aetate* cleared room for Catholics to look at their Muslim neighbors as people of genuine religious traditions inspired by the same Abrahamic tradition as their own. The Pontifical Council for Interreligious Dialogue (PCID) was founded to carry out dialogue with other religions, including Islam.

In the 1970s, Professor Mitchell felt called to enter this dialogue with the Buddhist world that he knew so well. In 1986, he became a consultant for the PCID and was a leader in its dialogue with Buddhism. Then came 9/11. And Professor Mitchell faced the world of doom and gloom that was shrouding the earth. The advocates of a "clash of civilizations" ruled out any possibility of dialogue, reconciliation, or a search for common ground. But, it was in this environment that Professor Mitchell decided to turn his attention to addressing this situation in the West by working with Muslims in order to build a more peaceful world.

In the meantime, American universities had about half a million Muslim students. Out of this new reality was born the Muslim Students Association of the United States and Canada in 1963. This organization was later transformed into the Islamic Society of North America (ISNA), the largest and oldest Muslim umbrella organization in America. This provided an opportunity to nourish a new Muslim community in a pluralist democracy far away from our own Muslim dictators and human rights violators.

It was a new identity with a new potential for bridge building. Our interfaith alliances, partnerships, and cooperation at the grassroots, national, and international levels with the U.S. Conference of Catholic Bishops, the National Council of Churches, the Union of Reform Judaism, and other religious organizations helped us build trust and confidence in a religiously pluralistic society. Since our ISNA headquarters is in Indiana, Professor Mitchell was invited to our dialogue meetings that were cosponsored by the U.S. Conference of Catholic Bishops. Professor Mitchell became our brother whom we trust and love.

Our beloved Professor Mitchell reached out to the U.S. State Department with the idea of bringing Muslims and Christians together to carry out peacebuilding projects and exchanges in the areas of the world where terrorism was polluting Muslims. He called on us at ISNA to partner with him as well as with other universities and organizations. We met at Purdue University, where he was a professor, and committed ourselves to carrying forward the vision he presented to us.

He created the Indiana Center for Cultural Exchange (ICCE) and literally took his mission to Central Asia, the Middle East, North Africa, Thailand, and the Philippines, covering the whole span of the so-called Muslim world. He worked with both the younger and older generations of Muslims and persons of other faiths such as Buddhism and Christianity. His work provided and strengthened a longing for a religiously inspired, single human family, as well as peace and justice coming from our recognition of interconnected and shared beliefs of human brotherhood and sisterhood. The struggle to build a world of peace and justice is a continuing challenge. But we see in Professor Mitchell's religious vision, courage, and dedication a powerful inspiration for the coming generations.

February 26, 2020
Washington, DC

CHAPTER 1

A Journey into Interreligious Dialogue
A Calling

Interreligious dialogue begins with a journey of the mind and heart beyond the frontier of one's own religion into the landscapes of other religions. If one merely crosses a bridge of the *mind* into the *intellectual* landscape of the other, this journey will only produce an interreligious discussion. Dialogue comes from crossing a bridge of the *heart* into the *spiritual* landscape of the other, keeping what is precious in one's own religion to share with the other, while being open to receiving what the other has to share. Here we are talking about people meeting and dialoguing from the heart, which leads to a heartfelt personal and spiritual encounter. My experience at this level is that we discover our common commitment to create a more united and peaceful world through loving-kindness and compassion. This kind of dialogue is at the service of the world in which we live today. In this chapter, I wish to share my own journey that led me to enter the heart of interreligious dialogue.

During my early years growing up in San Diego, California, I attended a Congregational Church and enjoyed reading the

Bible, memorizing Bible verses, and being part of the community. But over time, I was more attracted to the California lifestyle. I stopped going to church, and my "spiritual" life was on the beach, in the mountains, or the desert.

Later, at San Diego State University where I studied philosophy, one of my professors was Ray Jordan, an early Zen Buddhist in California. I liked what he said about Buddhism and decided to practice Zen meditation, *zazen,* under his direction. The practice led me to a deeper quiet place within. This experience made me consider going to graduate school to study Buddhism.

By this time, I was married to my wife, Ann, who is Catholic, and we had a baby named Jim. Her faith made me wonder about God. So, I read books such as Rudolf Otto's *The Idea of the Holy,* and Mircea Eliade's *Sacred and the Profane.* One night, I took a walk by myself and saw my old Congregational Church. It reminded me of what Eliade wrote about sacred space; namely, it is a space where one may experience the Sacred—like a church, synagogue, or mosque. I approached the church, but it was locked.

As I stood there, I heard a voice say, "There is a window open behind you." I looked behind me and saw a series of small, high windows. I thought that I was imagining things. So to prove it, I walked over and touched the first window. It swung open. That scared me! However, I decided to enter the church and climbed up and through the window. Once inside, I went before the altar.

I had not prayed for years, so I just sat down in a lotus position before the altar. While I was sitting there, I noticed a light shining from my left onto a Bible near the altar. I got up and read a passage on the page to which the Bible was opened. It was about God punishing the Hebrews for not praying before undertaking a task.

So, I sat back down and prayed, "Is there anything more than this suffering I feel?" I was depressed at the time. Then, I saw a thick darkness come down from the roof. As it covered me, I felt a supernatural peace. I said to myself over and over: "What is this?" Then, the words came from within: "The peace that passes understanding." I cried. After some time, the thick darkness seemed to evaporate. So, I went to the window and climbed out, closing it behind me. I walked home in the dark. But, as I looked down the streets, I saw that the darkness was itself luminous—it seemed to be glittering with a kind of light I had never seen before. Later, I would discover that this particular experience is found in both Christianity and Buddhism.

Approaching graduation, I had two choices for where I could study Buddhism: the University of Hawai'i and the University of Washington. One evening, I decided to go to Pacific Beach and take a walk along the cliffs that I liked to visit in order to think about this choice. At one point, there was a vacant lot, and as I looked at it, I again saw a thick darkness. I went into it, which I could feel, and sat down on the edge of the cliff overlooking the ocean far below. Suddenly, the waves increased and splashed up to where I was sitting, which seemed impossible given the height of the cliff and the many large rocks below that were breaking the waves. But in the crashing, I heard the words: "Go to Hawai'i and study Buddhism, and I will bring you back to use you for my own purpose." I felt that God was telling me this—and the words have been imprinted in my mind down to today.

Buddhist Studies and the *Zendo*

Moving to Hawai'i was wonderful! I gained a love for the beauty of the island, the ocean, and the island culture. Our friends and my classmates were from all over Asia, which gave me an appreciation for their cultures and religions. My classes were mainly taught by Asian scholars such as David

Kalupahana for Theravada Buddhism and Kenneth Inada for Mahayana Buddhism. I also took courses in Sanskrit and Pali, as well as Chinese. These graduate seminars delved into the textual materials of the different forms of Buddhism in Asia with some comparative comments along the way.

Also, Ray Jordan had recommended that I join the Diamond Sangha of Bob Aitken in Hawai'i to develop my *zazen* (meditation). I went to the *Zendo* (meditation center) for the first time and was a bit surprised. We sat, we stood, we bowed, we chanted in Pali or Chinese, and at times, someone would strike a board with a wooden hammer, or ring bells, or hit a gong. We sat for long periods while someone with a long stick walked behind us, sometimes stopping and striking a person on both shoulders. We also did walking meditation between the sittings. I realized that I had entered a different—and at the time strange—religious landscape. But over time, I understood what was happening and found that there was a deep atmosphere of compassion and peace behind what was taking place. It seemed to be connecting me to a lineage into the ancient past. In this external and internal spiritual environment, I was enabled to go to a deeper place within me.

I learned important life lessons from Bob. Once, I had lunch with him and his wife Anne. I took it as a time to share my problems with him, hoping for wise advice. Each time, he would listen intently in a caring way, and then ask if I wanted more tea. I thought he was not appreciating the seriousness of my problems. But later, I realized this was a kind of dialogue pointing me toward an important truth: the acceptance of good and bad while living in the present moment. Zen sayings about this include, "While there are good days and bad days, every day is a good day!" or "Life is like falling from a waterfall. Sometimes we are upright. Sometimes we spin out of control. But we are always in the waterfall."

At the university, I eventually finished my courses, took my area exams, and wrote my dissertation on Rudolf Otto's phenomenology of religious consciousness of the East and West. My focus was on how religions develop "divination environments" wherein one can cultivate a religious consciousness of the Holy. Based on his study of mysticism, I proposed that such an environment should enable a person to "empty" the ego self and discover one's true self. To make this point, I drew from the writings of Japanese Buddhist Kyoto School members like Masao Abe and Keiji Nishitani, whom I had met at the Fifth East-West Philosophers Conference in 1969. Little did I know that in the Buddhist-Christian dialogue, I would work with both of them, especially Abe, who came to work with me for two years.

At the end of my four years at the Diamond Sangha, when I knew that I would be leaving soon, I practiced *zazen* with great intensity. On the last evening, I suddenly heard a leaf of a banana tree outside scrape across the screen of the window to the left of the altar. The sound was like a sudden and huge explosion! I looked up at the window, and it seemed like the whole cosmos was *in* the banana leaf, scraping the window. I felt a great peace and joy. As I got up to leave the *Zendo* for the last time, I wondered, *Is this in some way an experience of not just the banana leaf but of everything in the world?* I walked outside and looked out from the veranda where you could see all the way to Honolulu and the ocean. It was night, but the darkness was luminous and everything was glittering. I did not share this experience with Bob since for some reason, it seemed natural and ordinary. Later, I would connect this Zen experience with my experience walking home from my old Congregational Church at night and seeing the darkness and all things glittering with light.

At one point, I met Emma, the Kahuna (Hawaiian shaman) for one side of Oahu. She was a direct descendent of the head

Kahuna of the great King Kamehameha I. We became friends, and she taught me many things about the local spirits and the world of spirits, good and bad. I did not know it at the time, but what she taught me would later be helpful when I encountered such phenomena in Asia during dialogues. She once came to our house for dinner and to meet Ann. When we were going to leave Hawai'i for my position at Purdue University, we went to say goodbye to her. Ann had just learned that she was pregnant with our third child. We had a second son named David, so Ann wanted a girl. She did not mention this to Emma.

But Emma said to her, "You will have a baby girl, and I want you to name her *Kapuananionalani*. This word means 'beautiful child from the heavens.'"

Ann said, "If I have a girl, I will name her Kapuananionalani!" Indeed, months later, we had a daughter. Ann wrote her full name on the birth certificate: Kristen Ann Kapuananionalani Mitchell.

Conversion

Prior to receiving my doctorate, I accepted a position at Purdue University in West Lafayette, Indiana. Moving to Indiana from Hawai'i was not easy for me. Ann felt comfortable in the Midwestern community, but I missed my Buddhist connections, the life and culture in Hawai'i, and the ocean. So, I attended conferences on Buddhism held in other cities. At one, I met Geshe Sopa, who helped found the Buddhist Studies Program at the University of Wisconsin. He was the Dalai Lama's examiner, the person who examines his understanding of Buddhism as he was growing up. We became friends, and I visited him in Wisconsin where we spent hours talking about different topics related to Buddhism in particular and to living a spiritual life in general. It was not an intellectual conversation, but a religious dialogue from the heart. In the end, it helped me see that I was not in a good spiritual place in my life. I remember that with a deep sigh, Geshe said to me, "Perhaps you need to be raised in a monastery to live a spiritual life."

In fact, I found myself constantly struggling, and I became depressed again. I was also very agitated and was struggling with life. I took my frustrations out on Christianity in the classroom. I would constantly argue against Christianity when making comparisons with Eastern religions. Looking back, I realized that God was pulling me toward conversion, and I was fighting against it. In one of my classes, there was a woman auditing the course. She was an older devout Italian Catholic. Eventually, she got so upset with me that she went to a monastery of the Precious Blood Sisters and asked them to pray for my conversion.

Two weeks later, I walked by a building with a basement apartment. The door was ajar, and I looked inside. It was a den of drugs and sex. *It looks like the door to hell*, I thought, *and if I go on as I have, this may be where I end up*. In fact, a few nights later, I fell into despair and contemplated suicide. Only when faced with death did I think, *Maybe I should try Christianity*. Christianity seemed better than death. I asked Ann to call Fr. Leo Haigerty, whom I had met and liked, to come and baptize me. This is what one does in the Protestant tradition. While we waited, I went to our bedroom and lay on the bed. I thought maybe I should pray and remembered the Lord's Prayer. As I prayed, I had the sense that there were many persons praying with me. When I closed my eyes, I saw a line of people in front of me. I remember they included Bob Aitken, Emma, and Geshe Sopa. All were looking at me and smiling. Then, they looked to their right, and a light coming from that direction shined on their faces. Their smiles expressed joy. I looked in that direction and thought, *Now, I will see God*. But instead, I saw only darkness. But, I felt like I was turning my life in the right direction. The priest knocked on the door.

Fr. Leo explained to me that in the Catholic Church there is a period of preparation before being baptized. So, I began my official entry into the Church, and on August 27, 1974, I was baptized, confirmed, and received my first communion. Fr. Leo gave me a volume of the writings of the Apostolic Fathers who were converted by Peter, Paul, and John. He gave it to me so I could relate their lives and experiences to my own conversion in order to better understand and appreciate Christianity through their writings. I continued reading the Church Fathers up to Augustine. Although the next year was very difficult as my life seemed to be turned upside down, the one thing that was constant was God's love. People asked me what my experience was as a new Christian. All I could say was, "God loves me." Then, I would cry.

One day, I met Brother David Steindl-Rast, who was giving a lecture at St. Thomas Aquinas Church next to the Purdue campus. Fr. Leo arranged for me to take a walk with David, and I told him how difficult it was to concentrate on my work with everything going on inside. I said that I had a lot of questions like what is the Trinity, the role of Mary, etc. He replied with a question: "What is inside that building across the street?" I said I did not know. He said, "If we walk there, we can find out, but it takes time. So, when you arrive at the place where God wants you to understand something, He will present it to you. Just be content with what you do know, and leave the process in God's hands."

Soon after this, I met with Katagiri Roshi, who at the time was my Zen Master at a distance. I had been continuing to practice *zazen* after my conversion since I did not see any conflict with my new faith. I told him about my conversion and the advice Brother David had given me. He agreed that the advice was good. Then, he said, "Just remember you are walking on the back of a water buffalo. When you take a step forward, he is there under your feet always supporting you. Just have faith and go ahead one step at a time." He also said that to go ahead as a Catholic, I needed to let go of my Buddhism for a while. He raised his hand, spread out his fingers, and said:

> Religions are like fingers on a hand. If you jump from one fingertip to another, you never reach the deeper truth in the palm. Make a choice that until you die, you will go down one finger into the hand. If you follow the finger of a Christian spirituality, you will reach the truth. If I follow mine, we will meet in the palm, and we will be one.

I said that I had not yet found a Christian spirituality to practice. He said, "Just be patient and it will come to you." I would add that at the end of our visit, he met Fr. Leo and said to me, "He is enlightened! He lives his true self!"

Our new Italian Catholic friend who went to the sisters to pray for my conversion, Adele Colella, invited Ann and me to hear a person speak at our church about a Christian lay spirituality she thought I might like. Given my talks with Brother David and Katagiri Roshi, I was beginning to look for a spirituality. Ann and I went and listened to Carl Tomassin from the Focolare Center in Chicago. He told a story about the founder, Chiara Lubich, and her companions who began the Focolare spirituality of love and unity during World War II in the city of Trent, which was heavily bombed. They would meet in the bomb shelters with only the Gospels to read. Otherwise, they were tending to the poor and the wounded in the city. As I listened, I had the sense that Chiara's story of a spirituality of love and unity that embraces all humanity and nature while caring for those in need was in some way my future story too.

Later, I found similarities between the Focolare and Buddhism such as living in the present moment, being compassionate for each person one meets, emptying of self so Christ (like Buddha-nature) within us can work through us, tending to the suffering of others out of compassion, and especially living a relational unity that expresses the essential unity of life. The thought that came to mind was, *Maybe Katagiri Roshi was right in asking me to find a spirituality in which we could be united as brothers.* Also, this was a spirituality that Ann and I could live together and share with our children. That was important to me because I practiced Zen by myself. So, as a family, we joined the Focolare, and very importantly for me, I later found that the Focolare was deeply involved in interreligious dialogue.

Holy Hill

Over the following years, I considered participating in the new Global Buddhist-Christian dialogue. My first sabbatical began in the fall of 1977, so I consulted with my friend, Raimondo Panikkar, who was a noted scholar in the Christian-Hindu dialogue. He suggested that I prepare for being involved in the dialogue with Buddhism by studying Christian spiritualty at the Jesuit School of Theology at the Graduate Theological Union in Berkeley, California. I also received a grant from Lilly Endowment that required a practicum. I made arrangements for our family to stay at Loppiano, Italy, for three months. Loppinao is a small village in the hills of Tuscany, south of Florence, that is the site of the school of formation for the Focolare. It overlooks the Arno River Valley with the Vallombrosa Abbey on the hill across the valley. And, over the hills behind Loppiano is the Chianti region of Italy. My intention was to participate in the formation process of the Focolare spiritualty in Loppiano.

The Graduate Theological Union is on a hill above the Berkeley campus, so its site is called "Holy Hill." I was a visiting scholar, which allowed me to sit in whatever courses I wanted to take. I took Michael Buckley's course on John of the Cross and Ed Malatesta's course on the Spiritual Exercises. I also took courses on spiritualty from the Dominicans and the Franciscans. I found all the classes to be helpful in understanding Christian spirituality from different points of view. Plus, Dan O'Hanlon gave a class on the writings of Thomas Merton that gave me new ideas about the Buddhist-Christian dialogue. Raimondo was right. Holy Hill was the place for me.

Dan was also my spiritual director. I was going through the Dark Night of the Senses, and he was a wonderful guide through that difficult time.[1] He introduced me to the monastic tradition of *Lectio Divina*. He had found that Buddhists like this spiritual approach to scripture and found it similar to their own. One starts with *lectio,* or reading scripture. If one is moved by a passage, he or she stops and meditates *(meditatio)* quietly. If this reflection deepens into an affective state, then one would move to *oratio* or spontaneous prayer to God. If God stills one's mind and heart, then one would remain in that contemplation *(contemplatio)* that is not produced by the person but by God. Dan said that if this last stage did not happen, do not worry since it is up to God, not oneself. When any of the stages 2 to 4 subside, then one returns to reading more of the scripture. I found that this was very helpful and compared it to chanting and meditating scripture in Buddhism.

---

[1] See: Donald W. Mitchell, *My Dark Nights* (New York: Herder & Herder/Crossroad Publishing, 2021), pp. 1–57.

Over time during the Dark Night, I came to realize that a change was going on in my relationship to Jesus. Dan said that this is typical when God is preparing a person for a task. God wants the person to have a deep relation to Jesus that is necessary to carry out God's will. I assumed that this new task must be interreligious dialogue. Also, I became friends with Jim Connor, who was assistant novice master with Thomas Merton. He shared with me:

> In mystical darkness, we find Jesus Crucified to be embraced in the darkness and suffering. This enables us to reach out beyond our monastic walls to minister to humanity, and to be with Jesus suffering in humanity in prayer and action. So when a Dark Night comes, we need to trust in God's grace at work in us for the benefit of humanity. It takes time since God cannot change lives in one or a few experiences. Each digs deeper into our being until we become more of who we really are, our true self, the way God created us to be.

City on a Mountain Top

At the end of the semester, Ann and I and the kids left San Francisco to go to Loppiano in Italy for my practicum in spiritualty with the Focolare. As we left San Francisco, the Dark Night lifted. When we arrived in Loppiano, we were given an apartment in nearby Palazzolo that we shared with nightly guests of all kinds from families to Orthodox and Coptic monks. I was given a half-day job in a workshop reconditioning electric meters for the city of Florence. Our three children attended a local school near Loppiano with other children of the families who lived in Loppiano. The families in Loppiano were mainly farmers who tended the olive groves, grape vines, and wheat fields. In the afternoons after Mass and lunch, I met with Walter Hobe, who instructed me in the charism and spiritual life of the Focolare.

One day, Chiara Lubich, the founder of the Focolare, arrived in Loppiano, and we were invited to meet her. I remembered that the early Jesuits said that when they were in the presence of St. Ignatius, they could experience his charism: finding God in all things. They were not able to experience this charism so well when he was not with them. John of the Cross noted that a founder is like a "pane of glass" in whom one sees the charism given to him or her by God. This happened to me when we met Chiara for the first time.

As her car drove up, it seemed that a man was in the front seat. Then, as Chiara came over to us, I saw a man standing in front of me and looking at me. I was confused and thought to myself, *Chiara is a man!* Then, I heard these words internally: *I am neither man nor woman.* Those words suddenly made my whole being absolutely still. I looked at his face and noticed that there were lines on his forehead that were vertical, not horizontal like on regular faces. I thought of the crown of thorns. Then, when Chiara walked away, he followed. I thought, *Will I ever see you again?*

At that moment, he stopped and turned a little toward me and said, "Not like this."

Before Chiara left Loppiano, I wrote her a letter about my background with Buddhism and my desire to enter the Buddhist-Christian dialogue. Her response was a message encouraging me to pursue the dialogue by looking for what can unite us as brothers and sisters. She also asked me to write to her about Buddhist spirituality that would be useful during her trips to Asia.

As we lived the Focolare spirituality of love and unity, at one point, I began to feel called to be a married Focolarino; that is, a married person who takes the three promises and becomes a full member of the Focolare. The married Focolarini participate equally with the celibate Focolarini in the life and activities of the Focolare Movement. While I felt called to this vocation, I also felt a resistance as I did earlier with Christianity. So, I wrote a list of ten reasons why I should *not* become a married Focolarino. I shared them with Walter. He asked me, "Is there someone in Loppiano putting pressure on you to be a Focolarino?" I said no. Then, I realized that the pressure was from God inside me and, as usual, I was resisting.

The next day, I listened to a tape recording of one of Chiara's first companions named Giosi. She talked about how during the war, they gave everything to the poor, keeping only one dress each and one pair of shoes. They gave away their food, but more was brought to them from the countryside. They took the sick and wounded into their apartment to care for them. They were always given providence that kept them going. When I heard this, I thought of the passage, "Give and it will be given to you." Again, that seemed like a call from God. I sent a message to Chiara that I would become a married Focolarino. I felt that a burden I did not know was on my shoulders was lifted.

Once I made this choice, Ann and I and our children took some time to travel to other religious communities in Italy. We visited the Benedictines in Vallambrosa, who loved the Focolarini. The abbot took us on a tour and shared about their life as monastics along the way. We also visited the Franciscan monastery on La Verna, the mountain where St. Francis of Assisi received the stigmata. Friar Eugene, the abbot, left a meeting and took over an hour to show us around and talk about St. Francis. I asked him his impression of the Focolare, and he said, "The Focolare seeks to answer with the lives of its members, the Lord's Prayer: 'Thy will be done on earth as it is in heaven.'"

We took a short vacation in Assisi. It was like going back to the time of St. Francis, especially in the evenings when the other tourists were gone. I could sense peace everywhere. Chiara began her religious life as leader of the Third Order of St. Francis in the city of Trent before the war. The Focolare was in some ways born from the Franciscans. I felt in Assisi that God was calling me to dedicate my work in the Buddhist-Christian dialogue, especially to peacebuilding. This was the "purpose" he had for me.

After leaving Assisi, we drove to nearby Spello to look for Carlo Carretto, the famous spiritual writer and member of the Little Brother of Jesus, the order founded by Charles de Foucould. I had been impressed when years ago, I read about how Carretto lived in the Sahara Desert caring for the "least in the world." Little did I know that someday I would be in the Sahara on a dialogue of peacebuilding.

We only knew that he was at Spello living with a group of his brothers and sisters. We went to the run-down cemetery building where a local man said that Carretto lived. But an old woman answered the door and said he lived in a hermitage in the hills and that we should follow the "red arrows." It turned out that red arrows were painted on rocks and trees, leading us to the hermitage. I remember stopping at a stream and seeing a red arrow on the other side. Driving a small Italian car, it was a challenge to go forward . . . but we did. Eventually, we came to a small house where a woman was outside hanging out laundry. Her eyes were so radiant that I knew we had arrived.

We entered the house and asked for Brother Carlo. He came into the room and asked us why we had gone to so much trouble to find him. I told him about my conversion and that I had read his book, *Letters from the Desert*. His book had encouraged me to find a Christian spirituality. Being married with children, I was led by God to the Focolare. He said that he was happy we all had become "children of Chiara." He showed us his hermitage and the chapel in which was a powerful presence of God. We discussed spirituality and dialogue since he was with Muslims in the Sahara. As he talked, I felt the urge to dialogue with Muslims in the Sahara—and eventually, this would take place!

Returning to Loppiano, I asked which Buddhist groups were in dialogue with the Focolare in Asia. I was told that there is a strong connection between the Focolare communities in Thailand and the Buddhist followers of Ajahan Thong, whose monastery is outside Chang Mai. Also in Bangkok there are Buddhist friends of the Focolare. They send their youth to the large events in Rome put on by the Focolare, and many young Thai Buddhists visit Loppiano. In Thailand, the monks refer to Chiara as "Mother Chiara."

Another strong contact was in Japan with the modern Japanese Buddhist lay movement, the Rissho Kosei-kai. Chiara Lubich met Nikkyo Niwano, the founder of the Rissho Kosei-kai, and they became good friends. Their first meeting took place when Nikkyo Niwano was traveling to London to receive the Templeton Prize for Progress in Religion. Chiara Lubich had received the prize a few years earlier. Niwano invited Lubich to Tokyo where she shared her spiritual story to 10,000 members of the Rissho Kosei-kai leadership. Since then, the two movements have collaborated in different forms of social engagement, and there has been a number of Rissho Kosei-kai members visiting Loppiano for different lengths of time.

I met two Rissho Kosei-kai youths staying in Loppiano and visited with them for an afternoon. They said that they were integrated into the Loppiano community and were not just observers. One of the boys named Michio said:

> I feel at home here. This is really unusual because Italy is so different from Japan, especially the social interactions. But here, I am accepted just as I am, and I feel the freedom to be myself. There is an atmosphere of love. There seems to be a spiritual dimension that unites us, even if we might try to define it in different ways. My Christian friends also say that the dialogue of life we live together is not abstract or conceptual, but personal based on our deep friendship. So, it is the best way for them to understand Buddhism.

Turning to his friend, Masao, I asked, "What do you find in common here?" He replied:

> We both apply our faith to daily life. We both know that compassion is the core of our existence, but that these are not just inner states of mind. We both live our compassion in each moment as best we can, given our insights about the interconnectedness of life. All persons are our brothers and sisters and need our compassion.

A third strong contact with Buddhists was in Sri Lanka. The famous A. T. Ariyaratne founded a Buddhist village renewal movement called the Sarvodaya Shramadana Movement. *Sarvodaya* is a term coined by Gandhi to mean "the well-being of all." *Shramadana* means "the gift of sharing one's time and labor." Ariyaratne's movement seeks to live Buddhism by sharing both time and labor for the well-being of all. Members volunteer their time and efforts in very poor villages. They not only do projects, but also help the villagers and volunteers to cultivate friendships and to share in a way that fosters both personal awakening and social development. Besides reconstructing the villages, they seek to reconstruct the minds and hearts of the villagers through a spirituality that contributes to overcoming poverty and social ills. The Focolare has been working with Ariyaratne both in Sri Lanka and south India given the shared ideal of a more united world. Later, after returning to the United States, I would meet Ariyaratne at a Buddhist-Christian dialogue. We felt a strong bond once he knew I was part of the Focolare. He was an amazing man totally dedicated to peacebuilding in his country, and he has always remained a model for me.

Hindus in Tuscany

Every week, there were many visitors who came to Loppiano from all over Italy and from other parts of Europe. They would arrive in bright-colored tour buses for a program and luncheon the community put on each Sunday. One week, we had two buses arrive in the middle of the week with guests from a little further away—from India. They were all from Gandhi Ashrams throughout India and were visiting religious communities in Europe to see how they are structured and how they support themselves. In India, they practice a socially engaged form of Gandhian Hindu spirituality in what is called their Village Grant Program. My

Hindu-Christian encounter with them taught me an extremely valuable lesson about the world of interreligious dialogue.

Our Indian guests arrived late one afternoon. My own thought at the time was that the persons I greeted would probably like to talk to me about religion. Since I teach Hinduism, I thought that I would be the best person with whom they could have a dialogue. As they got off the bus, I found myself distracted as I tried to remember some of the finer points of Vedanta and some of the comparative ideas that had recently surfaced in the Hindu-Christian dialogue. Then, a middle-aged man came over and introduced himself: "Hello. My name is Raj," he said.

I replied, "My name is Don. I am from the United States." We shook hands. Then, I took a breath and started what I thought would be a dialogue: "So, you belong to a Gandhi Ashram in India. That must mean you are a Hindu." Raj nodded but looked at me with a kind of questioning glance. "You know, I teach Hinduism in an introductory religion course. I really like the section on Vedanta. I assume that you agree with one of the three major positions of the Vedanta tradition. Which one do you consider correct? The Vedanta of Sankara, Ramanuja, or Madva?" As I was speaking, Raj's questioning glance was replaced with a kind of blank stare.

When I had finished my question, Raj said, "You know, I am not really sure about those kinds of things. Excuse me a moment." With that, he walked over to one of his companions, and I found myself alone.

As I stood there, I could feel my disappointment turning into anger. *What is wrong with this guy? Doesn't he know he is passing up an opportunity to dialogue with someone who knows about Hinduism?* Then, I saw how many of the guests were gravitating to people like Roberta. Roberta is a very kind Focolarina. Ann sees her for spiritual direction, and I have gotten to know and respect her for being a down-to-earth kind of person. But in this instance, I felt jealous. *Why did these people prefer to speak to her and not to me? She does not know anything about Hinduism,* I thought. It even seemed as though some of the women speaking to Roberta had known her all their lives. Later, I asked Roberta if she had met these women before. She said that this was the first time she had met them.

Our guests only stayed a short time but were to return for a longer tour of the community the next day. Back home at our guesthouse, I thought about my failure to spark anything resembling a dialogue with Raj. Maybe Roberta had taught me a lesson about the dialogue of the heart and not just the mind. Roberta's simple, sincere, and compassionate connection with our guests produced a heartfelt rapport that all my knowledge could not achieve. Obviously, Raj had wanted to get to know me since he came over and introduced himself. Maybe I just needed to get to know our guests and serve them with the love I saw in Roberta.

I decided to have a different attitude the next day. As soon as the bus arrived, I simply put myself at the service of our guests. I did so without an agenda or ulterior motive. After finding out what they wanted to see and do, I drove them around the community, putting myself at their disposal. They were especially interested in the cloistered nuns who live in a convent on the property. They could not believe that the sisters never left their cloister. But what really touched them deeply was a visit with the families who work in the cooperative. Some of them live together in a large farmhouse that had been rebuilt into a number of apartments. The children had prepared a skit for the guests and also sang some songs.

At one point, Raj ran over to me, excited. Gesturing with his arms in the air, he said, "You can tell if a spirituality is true by the way the children are. The fruit of a people's spirituality can be seen in the lives of their children. These children are really free. Now, I can accept that your spirituality is from God!" In fact, after this visit to the families, some of the women in the group asked if they could send their own children to live in Loppiano for a period of time.

That evening, we went to the women's center for dinner and a program about Loppiano. At dinner, I sat at a table across from a Focolarina, who said as she sat down: "Let's just keep Jesus in our midst." I agreed and again thought to myself, *Perhaps dialogue is sparked by the heart rather than the head.*

At one point during the meal, the Hindu elder at the table looked up from his plate and said, "I have learned how to love here. Love involves an asceticism, a dying to yourself, your ego, in order to care for others. This kind of love sets free the spirit of God between us."

Then, an older woman said, "When I was fourteen, I was married. But by sixteen, I was a widow. With no place to go, I entered a Gandhi Ashram and worked with the Village Grant Program. We have been traveling for many weeks now, and I am tired. But here, I found a kind of love that is new. It makes me feel young again. It gives me hope, and I feel at home."

With that, the elder Hindu looked up from his soup with tears in his eyes and said, "You know? I *really* feel the presence of God here." Then, he looked down again. The other guests nodded, and no one spoke after that. We finished our meal in silence.

After dinner, there was a short program of entertainment. In one of the songs, there was mention of the Cross. The Hindu woman from our table turned to me and asked what the crucifix represents. I told her about the "self-emptying" of Jesus on the Cross out of love for humankind, and that his death for our sake led to his resurrection. She responded enthusiastically, "That is like our experience of death and new life in our spirituality! When we die to our small and limited ego, we find that within us is another self, our Atman or true self. This true self is the very divine life of God itself."

I replied, "There is a passage in our scripture that says, 'It is no longer I who live, but Christ within me who lives.'" She smiled and nodded her head in agreement.

It was during my time in Loppiano that I came to understand that deep dialogue must come from the heart, not just the head. You cannot just sit down at a table with strangers of another faith and start talking. That just leads to discussion, not a deep dialogue. I remember seeing this happen once when a religious organization decided to "get into dialogue." People sat down at the table, talked for a while, and got up and left. My impression was that no real connection remained after that encounter. When our guests left Lopianno, there was a deep and substantial connection that remained in all of us. We really felt like we were spiritual brothers and sisters, fellow pilgrims on a journey into the Truth. Later, I heard that the Focolares in India had established relations with Gandhian communities.

The experience of dialogues in Loppiano reminded me of a time when I spoke to the Shin Buddhist Bishop, Rev. Fujitani, at a Buddhist Study Center when I was at the University of Hawai'i. I asked him how an early Buddhist-Christian collaboration in Hawai'i had started. This interfaith group was known at the time as a model for interreligious dialogue. Bishop Fujitani said:

> One day, I met the Catholic Bishop of Honolulu on the golf course. We played a round, and by the 18th hole, we had gotten to know and like each other. We became golfing buddies. The Catholic Bishop later introduced me to

some other religious leaders in Hawai'i who also played golf. Soon, we were all playing together and developed heartfelt friendships. We would dialogue spontaneously after playing. One day, a Protestant minister of a small church had a zoning problem. He felt like his community was being treated unjustly and was having trouble getting the matter taken care of properly by the state government. So, we all decided to go together to visit the governor of Hawai'i about this problem. When we went into his office, you could see the governor looking at each of us one at a time, adding up in his head the votes we represented. The zoning problem was taken care of the next day. It was our heartfelt friendships that began our dialogue of action.

At the end of our stay in Italy, we went to Rome. We stopped first in Vatican City and went to the Sistine Chapel and from there to St. Peters Basilica. Ann and the kids went up to the top of the dome. But I am afraid of heights, so I sat quietly in one of the pews near the main altar. As I prayed, I sensed that each prayer was a true and pure expression of my needs, and that each was heard with seriousness. I sensed the communion of saints with me and felt that Mary saw I was tired from the trip and the heat in Rome. I closed my eyes and fell sound asleep sitting up for the first time in my life. When I woke up, I felt like I was at *home* . . . in *my* house. I thought of the long journey that led me to my true home. I wept. When Ann and the kids came back, we went out on the steps and took out our sack lunches. A guard came over and said, "You cannot eat on the steps of St. Peters!"

I replied, "But this is our home." He made an Italian shrug and walked away. I learned that all rules in Italy are just suggestions.

The next day, we drove out to Castel Gandolfo to the general audience with Pope Paul VI. He seemed very old and tired, but at the same time, I sensed a certain holiness. I remember that he said something like, "Now you are traveling on vacation. You should ask yourself the question: 'Where am I going?'" I felt that he was asking me that question. Afterward, we had lunch on the patio of a small café. It had vines covering the entire patio area that all came from one root. Every time I go to Castel Gandolfo, I always eat at that restaurant.

On our way home, we stopped in London. There, I visited Ven. Saddhatissa, a Sri Lankan scholar of Theravada Buddhism and director of the London Buddhist Vihara. We had met at a talk on the Buddhist-Christian dialogue in Rome. In London, we spent an afternoon talking about Buddhism and its dialogue with Christianity. Our conversation was constantly being interrupted by the telephone ringing. Saddhatissa would answer the phone and treat the caller with great kindness, giving him or her as much time as he or she needed. By what I heard of these telephone conversations, I could tell that Saddhatissa was being a pastor to troubled persons in his community. Once when he put the receiver down, I asked him: "How much of your time each day is devoted to this kind of work?" Saddhatissa replied with a laugh:

> Most of my time while here in the office is devoted to helping people with problems. Most Buddhist monks

are "temple monks," working in cities with people. Very few are "forest monks" who devote themselves just to meditation. You know, *dukkha,* or the dissatisfactory condition of human existence, is not just a philosophical idea. We all have our personal *dukkha;* it is a universal reality shared in different ways by everyone. When I hear a person expressing his or her *dukkha,* my practice is for the good of that person. These phone calls are my Buddhist practice of loving-kindness and compassion.

We completed our conversation by both agreeing to be united at a distance as we practice loving-kindness and compassion from the heart in the world of the Buddhist-Christian dialogue for the good of humankind and all creation.

CHAPTER 2

Dialogues of the Mind and Heart

While my involvement in interreligious dialogue began in Italy, after returning home in 1978, I spent five years researching the topic, and the Buddhist-Christian dialogue in particular. I also studied texts on Buddhist and Christian spiritualties. But, before presenting my early dialogues that followed these studies, I need to make clear that it was not only the studies themselves that guided my life of dialogue. It was the Dark Night on Holy Hill that deepened my inner relationship with God, and especially with Jesus, and brought about the spiritual foundation for my life of dialogue. Below my mind and my heart, there was something more than me, deeper than me, something that included those with whom I dialogued, and all of humankind and nature too. It was this infinite horizon, this divine ground that embraces all because that One, that Love, that Unity *is* all. To use a Buddhist metaphor, it is like water below and in all the waves of existence.

Dialogues and Encounters with His Holiness the Dalai Lama

The first dialogue I had was with His Holiness the Dalai Lama in 1981. His Holiness would often visit the Tibetan Cultural Center that was founded by his brother, Professor Thublen J. Norbu, at Indiana University in 1979. The Dalai Lama would give formal teachings. For example, he gave teachings on important Buddhist texts like *The Heart Sutra* and *Lamp to the Path to Enlightenment*. He would also present public talks on topics relating to living Buddhism today like "Facing Today's Challenges with Wisdom and Compassion" and "Compassion, the Source of Enlightenment." I was so impressed with His Holiness's focus on compassion of the heart that in 1981, with the help of the Office of Tibet, I arranged a meeting with him at Indiana University.

When I entered the living room of the suite in the Memorial Union where we were scheduled to meet, I saw that all the walls of the room had stuffed animal heads! I wondered why they would put the Dalai Lama in such a room. Then, he appeared in the doorway to other rooms and motioned for me to come to him. He led me to a smaller room, noting that he does not go into the living room. I was moved by his presence, simplicity, and kindness. I felt that I was walking out of a room of killing into a room of compassion.

After I shared the private things I wanted to tell him, I presented my plans to become involved in the Buddhist-Christian dialogue. He then began asking me questions. He was interested in my involvement in the Focolare and asked if they worked with youth. I told him about the youth branch of the Focolare for different age groups. He became very animated as he asked me more questions about youth. Then, he sat silent and said, "This is one of the most important things a religion can do today, to teach them compassion and love for others. Because in the near future, children will do terrible things, even killing other children." To tell the truth, at that point in time, I did not think that what he said would happen. Eighteen years later, on April 20, 1999, Columbine happened. And that was just the beginning.

At one point, he paused and then told me that I was on the right path in the Focolare spirituality. The only thing he said that he would suggest from his spirituality was that I become a vegetarian. He made it clear that it was not a necessity but would be good for me. Then, he said something that has influenced the rest of my life. He said, "How we treat *any* living being affects the way we treat *all* living beings." It took many years, but at one point in the jungle in India, I understood and never harmed a living creature from then on. After more conversation, we embraced and I departed with a deep sense of peace that I could not explain. But, I also had a sense that we would meet again.

Twelve years later, we met in 1993 at the 100th anniversary of the Parliament of the World's Religions in Chicago. There was a panel organized by Monastic Interreligious Dialogue (MID) based on my recent book, *Spirituality and Emptiness*.[1] MID was founded by the Benedictine order, at the request of the Vatican, in order to carry out intermonastic dialogues with Buddhism. His Holiness the Dalai Lama was on the panel. At the end of the discussion, he said that he felt like the time was right for a week retreat for monastics, Buddhists, and Catholics to share more deeply their spiritualties and to deepen their relationships as brothers and sisters. This request fit with a central goal of the Catholic Church's interreligious dialogues at that

---

1 Donald W. Mitchell, *Spirituality and Emptiness: The Dynamics of Spiritual Life in Buddhism and Christianity* (Mahwah, NJ: Paulist Press, 1991).

time: mutual understanding and appreciation. But MID added the deeper aspect of a mutual fraternity as monks and nuns. For His Holiness, dialogue was obviously not just a matter of the mind but must come from the heart. He suggested that it be held at Gethsemani Abbey where his friend Thomas Merton had lived.

MID, led by Sr. Margaret Mary Funk, O.S.B., asked me to help them organize the dialogue retreat since they had never held one before. They also wanted me to help them invite important Buddhists from around the world. I was honored to do so. The now famous Gethsemani Encounter, which I will discuss later in this chapter, took place in 1996. Jeffery Hopkins, a Tibetan Buddhist scholar and one of the English-language interpreters for His Holiness, and I gave the joint opening talks. Jeffery spoke about "Nirvana, Buddhahood, and the Spiritual Life;" and I spoke about "God, Creation, and the Spiritual Life." When I was done, His Holiness stood up and put his palms together and raised them over his head. Later, he came up to me and said, "If God is infinite Love as you say, then I believe in God." In return, I asked him to explain Nirvana to the whole group. He said that he would give a formal teaching about Nirvana. I will summarize his teaching below. But more important to me is that he came to me to talk about divine Love.

We spoke a few other times at Gethsemani, but what really impressed me is something he did many times during the retreat. Each time we walked from the chapter room where the dialogue was held in the middle of the monastery, we would pass through the church. As we did, he would always stop in front of the tabernacle and bow very low in devotion. On the last day, as he passed by for the final time, he did the same. But, as he approached the door, he turned around and faced the tabernacle and waved goodbye with a radiant smile on his face. I still have a picture of that moment in my mind.

After the Gethsemani Encounter, Fr. Jim Wiseman, O.S.B. and I published the talks and the dialogues in a book entitled *The Gethsemani Encounter*.[2] As we prepared the manuscript, I was surprised at how many times His Holiness gave words of advice to both Buddhists and Christians during the encounter. Working with His Holiness and the Office of Tibet, I edited *Spiritual Advice for Buddhists and Christians*,[3] which was translated into a number of languages.

In 2003, we met again at the Tibetan Cultural Center where he appeared with Muhammad Ali. Muhammad Ali was a follower of Warith Deen Muhammad, the son of the founder of the Nation of Islam, Elijah Muhammad. W. D. Muhammad had become close friends with Chiara Lubich and invited her to speak at the Malcolm Shabazz Mosque in Harlem in 1997. She did so, and a pact of unity was made between W. D. and Chiara. A few years later, there was a meeting of 7,000 members of the Focolare and African-American Muslim communities who gathered to hear both Chiara and W. D. That meeting in 2000 was my first encounter with W. D. Muhammad. Three years later, W. D. Muhammad and I sat together watching Muhammad Ali and the Dalai Lama speak about religion and peace.

After the event, there was a private audience with His Holiness to which I was invited. On the way there, I had a chance meeting with Muhammad Ali. His guards kept me and my son Paul away. But then, I heard his voice calling us to come to him. We did and he posed with us for pictures. I would meet him many years later in another kind of dialogue. The audience

---

2 Donald W. Mitchell and James Wiseman, O.S.B., eds., *The Gethsemani Encounter: A Dialogue on the Spiritual Life by Buddhists and Christian Monastics* (New York: Continuum, 1999).

3 His Holiness the Dalai Lama, *Spiritual Advice for Buddhists and Christians*, ed. Donald W. Mitchell (New York: Bloomsbury Academic, 1998).

with His Holiness was somber. Professor Norbu had passed away, and the Dalai Lama was reflecting on the loss of his brother, his own age, his future death, and what it would mean for Tibet. The discussion was quiet and personal.

The last time I was with His Holiness was at Purdue University. Some years before that meeting, I had met Arjia Thubten Lobsang Rinpoche, director of the Tibetan Mongolian Cultural Center.[4] Arjia Rinpoche was at one time the Abbot of Kumbum Monastery in Tibet. But, he escaped from Tibet and found asylum in the United States. In 2006, at the request of the Dalai Lama, he became director of the Center in Bloomington. We have had a close friendship over the years, and he helped facilitate the Dalai Lama's visit to my university. I was able to introduce him to my family backstage and greet him one last time.

Then one day, His Holiness's youngest brother, Tendzin Choegyal, came to our house for dinner. During the dinner conversation, I asked him if he thought his brother was really an emanation of Avalokiteshvara. I should mention that Buddhists following in the Sutra tradition believe in bodhisattvas who are on the path to full Buddhahood. They reside in the celestial realms of Buddhas, while assisting people in this world out of compassion. Avalokiteshvara is the Bodhisattva of Compassion and is thought to be at the tenth and final stage of the path to Buddhahood. But from a Tantric point of view, especially in Tibetan Buddhism, Avalokiteshvara is the embodiment of the compassion of all Buddhas, and thus is a fully enlightened Buddha. Tendzin thought for a while and said:

> On the one hand, I wish he were not since it would mean I might be able to eventually achieve what he has

---

4 The Dalai Lama had changed the name of the center to the Tibetan Mongolian Cultural Center.

become. But, there are many things that indicate that he is. For example, when he was brought to the Potala Palace as a child of two years old, he entered the room of the previous Dalai Lama. He went over to a dresser and pulled out a box with the false teeth of the previous Dalai Lama and said, "These are mine."

Tenzin expanded on his answer by describing how this kind of thing also happened when the Dalai Lama was found:

Our family lived in a small and poor village named Taktser in far northeastern Tibet. When the previous Dalai Lama, Thupten Gyatso, was sitting in state, his head was found to be turned to the northeast. Also, the Regent went to a sacred lake and saw in it the Tibetan letters Ah, Ka, and Ma. He also saw a three-storied monastery with a turquoise and gold roof and a small house with unusual guttering. So, the search party was sent and went to Kumbum Monastery in the northeastern province of Amdo given the letters Ah and Kh. They searched the villages looking for a house and eventually found our house with the unusual guttering. The search team presented to my brother a number of items that belonged to the previous Dalai Lama as well as other items that did not belong to him. He picked out the ones belonging to the previous Dalai Lama saying, "It is mine."

An Academic Dialogue in Hawai'i

It was not until 1984 that I first attended an academic Buddhist-Christian dialogue. It was the Second International East-West Religions in Encounter Conference hosted by the University of Hawai'i. I felt that it was a bit like a homecoming. I even went back to Bob Aitken Roshi's *Zendo* where I had practiced for four years. After the sitting, I had a quiet conversation with Bob and his wife Anne. At the conference, I presented "The 'Place' of the Self in Christian Spirituality: A Response to the Buddhist-Christian Dialogue."[5] Later, when the famous Masao Abe of the Kyoto School in Japan presented a paper on God and Emptiness, Hans Küng made a response that was misinformed. I brought the two together and helped Hans understand Abe's notion of Emptiness. Hans invited me to lunch. As we had lunch, he suddenly realized I was not a Buddhist. "I thought you were a Buddhist," he said. I told him I was a Catholic. He replied, "I would not have taken you to be a Catholic since you seem to have very close relations to the Buddhists here."

I responded, "That is the point of a dialogue of the heart." We became good friends and met for years at other dialogues. Once he came to my home for dinner, and another time I went with him to celebrate his birthday.

---

5 "The 'Place' of the Self in Christian Spirituality: A Response to the Buddhist-Christian Dialogue," *Japanese Religions* (Vol. 13, No. 3: December, 1984) pp. 2–26.

At this conference, Masao Abe told John Cobb, the famous theologian, that he wanted me to be part of a new dialogue group they had started called "The Abe-Cobb Group." It was made up of Buddhist scholars and Christian theologians. Members included John B. Cobb, Schubert M. Ogden, David Tracy, Marjorie Suchocki, Hans Küng, John Berthrong, John Hick, David Chappel, Langdon Gilkey, Gordon Kaufman, and Rosemary Ruether on the Christian side. On the Buddhist side were Masao Abe, Rita Gross, David Kalupahana, Ryunsei Takeda, Taitetsu Unno, Francis Dojin Cook, Chatsumarn Kabilsingh, Venerable Yifa, and Judith Simmer Brown. Abe had realized that the group needed someone who knew both sides of the dialogue to be a kind of bridge for better mutual understanding. I accepted the invitation, and we met annually for years. At one point, the funding ran out, and I was able to obtain a large grant from the Lilly Endowment to keep it going under the name The International Buddhist-Christian Theological Encounter.

It was also at the Hawai'i conference that David Chappel and others of us began discussing the founding of a society and a journal. This eventually led to the Society for Buddhist-Christian Studies and its journal, published by the University of Hawai'i Press, *Buddhist-Christian Studies*.

Dialogues in Japan

The dialogue in Hawai'i led to invitations to Buddhist and Christian organizations and universities in Japan and Hong Kong. In 1986, Ann and I went to Kyoto, Japan. I was very much influenced by the teachings of Shi'ichi Hisamatsu (1889–1980), the Zen Master of Masao Abe and the founder of the FAS Society that is related to the famous Kyoto School of Buddhist philosophy. So, I was happy to speak at an evening meeting of the FAS Society in the Shokokuji Buddhist Monastery complex that was founded in 1382. Geshen Tokiwa, a member of FAS, guided me through the darkness and cold with snow coming down. The buildings did not have lights, so we walked to the meditation hall in the dark only able to see the shapes of the monastic buildings around us that seemed like giant figures in the darkness. The meditation hall had windows all around but without windowpanes so the cold wind and snow blew on us all the time. We did *zazen* in a circle on the wooden floor. Then, I read my paper as I brushed away snowflakes. I could see my breath as I read and felt like I was back in the rigors of Zen training.

The paper was entitled "Unity and Dialogue: A Christian Response to Shin'ichi Hisamatsu's Notion of FAS." *F* stands for "Formless Self." Our "original" Formless or true self is not "formed" by our daily life but always remains pure within to be discovered and lived. The goal for Hisamatsu and his disciples is to discover by Zen practice one's true self. The *A* stands for "All Humankind." This refers to living a deep unity of compassion with all humankind. And the *S* stands for "Superhistoricity." This refers to the fact that by realizing our true self and living in deep compassion and unity within all humanity, we can transform history into the super-history of a united and peaceful world.

I presented Chiara Lubich's spirituality that leads to discovering the Trinitarian Unity of Life/Love that is within us. Thereby, we can also realize that this dynamic Unity of Life/Love within is also present in all humanity and all creatures. With this inner realization, those following this spirituality seek to give birth to a united and peaceful world. Chiara's spirituality leads to an experience of a "fire" of Love that can burn away all divisions and contributes to the unity of all humankind. Therefore, Chiara's spiritualty involves a dialogue of the heart with other religions to further a more united world. The FAS members asked a number of questions. At the end of the meeting, the leadership decided that my talk would be the first paper to be published in the *FAS Society Journal* by a non-Buddhist.[6]

Also in Kyoto, I presented a paper at Ryukoku University, a Pure Land Buddhist institution. Unlike Zen, Pure Land Buddhism focuses on faith in Amida Buddha for spiritual growth due to grace, and for birth in the Pure Land, the celestial realm of Amida Buddha, after death. My paper was on "Shinran's Religious Philosophy and Christian Mysticism."[7] Shinran was the founder of a sect of Pure Land Buddhism in the eleventh and twelfth centuries. My focus was on the mystical elements related to faith in both Christianity and Pure Land Buddhism.

The person who invited me to Ryukoku University was Professor Ryusei Takeda, who was also a member of the Abe-Cobb Group. He took Ann and me on a tour of their famous Buddha Hall and Dharma Hall in Kyoto. Ann and I were both very moved by the devotion given to Amida Buddha and the beautiful atmosphere in the ancient halls. At one point while looking at the statue of Amida Buddha, Ryusei said that he was a victim of the atomic bomb in Hiroshima. He was one of those children who jumped into the river to try to escape the burning. Afterward, he always asked himself, "Why did this happen to me? Why couldn't I have been in the countryside?" He was shunned for his burns since the Japanese always want pure light skin.

---

6 Donald W. Mitchell, "Unity and Dialogue: A Christian Response to Shin'ichi Hisamatsu's Notion of FAS," *FAS Society Journal* (Spring 1986), pp. 6–9.

7 Donald W. Mitchell, "Christian Mysticism and Shinran's Religious Philosophy," *The Shinshugaku Journal of Studies in Shin Buddhism* (74: June, 1986) pp. 27–45 [in Japanese].

The priests said, "This is your karma. You have to accept it." He could not. So, one day, he went to the temple we were in and kneeled before this statue of Amida Buddha. He surrendered himself to Amida and prayed for help. Then, he felt the love of Amida Buddha for him just as he was. That love entered his heart, and only then could he love and accept himself as he was. Ann said, "And now you are the most loving Japanese man I have met in Japan!"

One of my dialogues of the heart in Japan was with the famous Keiji Nishitani (1900–1990). He was a disciple of Kitaro Nishida, the founder of the Kyoto School. He was sent by Nishida to study with Martin Heidegger and was the leader of the Kyoto School from 1943 to 1964. When I visited him with Geshen Tokiwa, Nishitani was in the midst of mourning the death of his wife. We gathered in a small room with the rest of the house decorated in the mourning tradition. Here is a part of our dialogue:

GT: I met Professor Mitchell two years ago at an encounter where I presented a paper on Mary and Maya. He and I had a good dialogue about this since he belongs to the Work of Mary, otherwise known as the Focolare. This was the beginning of our friendship.

KN: I know the founder of the Focolare, Chiara Lubich. I read about her and also read her writings. You know [to Tokiwa] she was in Trent, Italy, during the World War II, and during bombings, she went to the bomb shelters. There she had her conversion.

DM: In your writings, you often speak of the movement from "self-centeredness" on the "field of consciousness" to "other centeredness" on the "field of Emptiness." It seems to me that this is achieved by what you call "making oneself empty" that enables one to live lovingly for the other.

KN: Yes.

DM: My question is this: If people discover together their true other-centered selves and live together in this way, would this make our true "Home-Ground," to use your word, of Love and Unity more evident in the world? Would this bring into the world what you call a "field of force" that would gather and unify humanity?

KN: Yes. And, when we attain deeper realization of the depth of this Home-Ground of Unity, we find the fundamental truth of community, of I-thou relations. When each person can attain that true Unity within oneself, he or she discovers mutual interpenetration, or what you call Trinitarian interpenetration. This is our fundamental way of being . . . Unity/Love. Here each person can realize his or her trueself. To discover our true self is at the same time the realization of true Unity. It is, in fact, the "self-realization of the Unity itself."

DM: If the realization of Unity is really the "self-realization of Unity itself," then it cannot be a product of our will alone. It must be established on the basis of Emptiness or God.

KN: What is the "place" of God? When a community is centered around Christ or Buddha, they become Christian or Buddhist churches or sanghas separate from each other. Today, we need a broader foundation that includes all religions, that makes a place where all religions can enter communication in a way that they did not have in the past . . . a deeper perspective where we can see each other as loving brothers and sisters. Such a new horizon has become a necessity. What is needed is unity, one world with every heart and every hearth, focolare. Hearts and hearths! The heart in the center of each person. The hearth is the center of the whole human family.

DM: In the past, Buddhists and Christians have searched for the true self or God in one's heart. This will always be essential. But, you are saying that today, we also need to seek the fundamental unity within all humankind. We need a spirituality that seeks not only a deeper unity in the heart, but in the hearth that unites the family of humankind.

KN: Yes, that is important.[8]

A second dialogue of the heart was with Kobori Nanrei Sohaku (1918–1992), Abbot of Ryokoin, a subtemple of Daitoku-ji founded in 1396. It was arranged by Fredrik Spier from the NCC Center for the Study of Japanese Religions. Kobori Roshi was a famous Rinzai Zen Master. We met in his subtemple one afternoon.

KS: So, you are involved in the Buddhist-Christian dialogue. This is very important and will be carried on in the next centuries. This dialogue needs to be carried out from both the scholarly side and the side of practice. *Bukkyo* means "teaching," and *Buppo* means the "Dharma" or "Essence of the Truth" that has no form. Scholars are just concerned with the words of the teachings. Going beyond the words to the Dharma is clearly the task of Zen meditation. Is there a similar process in Christianity?

---

8 Excerpted from "Compassionate Endurance: Mary and the Buddha: A Dialogue with Keiji Nishitani," *Bulletin of the Vatican Secretariat for Non-Christians,* Vol. 21, No. 3 (1986): 296–300.

DM: Yes. There are stages of spirituality that recollect and then quiet the mind beyond words. Then, there is contemplation that is not achieved by the person but by God at the depth of the person. There, one finds the Truth beyond words. One feels Love and Peace and Thankfulness.

KS: Hakuin said that when he reached the Dharma Essence, it was in the darkness of night where there was nobody, and he danced by himself. Just danced. The Dharma was so simply present in him that there could not be any words . . . just dancing joyfully. After that, some unknown sense wells up, and one feels gratitude. Now this is an interesting conversation. This is mutual illumination and respect. I also believe that a person reaches the depth of one's Essence by breathing out. In Genesis, we read that God breathed out and Adam became a living being. This breathing out of God is the Holy Spirit. The Buddha talked about "concentration on breathing out." There is a link between breathing out and the spirit helping us reach a deeper level, the very basis of our being.

DM: To me, the essence of God is *kenosis* or self-emptying Love in the Trinity where the Holy Spirit is the breath of Love. God is breathing us at our deepest core or center with the Spirit of Love. If we settle into the deepest part of ourselves, what we call our soul, we find God keep breathing us with all humanity and creation. In my prayer life, I no longer do pure *zazen*. But I find myself doing *zazen* breathing. It helps me settle into a deeper place within myself. It really is automatic when I pray.

KS: *Zazen* is not physical form. If what you do is based on this deep concentration with the aid of Zen breathing, then it is a Christian expression of *samadhi*. Samadhi is not the monopoly of Buddhism. When spring comes, several different flowers bloom: plum in white, cherry in pink, and dandelion in yellow. But spring is the distinctionless source shared with all the flowers. No distinction in spring, but flowers differ. When you pray deeply, you have no consciousness of Christianity. When I sit in deep Samadhi, there is no consciousness of Buddhism. In true religion, there is deep, quiet, and clear Love. When I am truly Buddhist and you are truly Christian, then we can respect each other from a deep religious level.

DM: I would like to discuss some thoughts about suffering. When Jesus was dying on the Cross, he cried out, "My God, my God, why have you forsaken me?" In his passion, he identified with the suffering of all persons, past, present, and future. In his cry, we hear that he felt separated from God, the ultimate "Home Ground" of all to use Nishitani's words. In my spirituality, when we suffer, we go deeply within ourselves and embrace the presence of Jesus Forsaken, since in his passion he became one with all our sufferings. There, we find inner peace and compassion in our suffering. The paradox is that the peace/love does not negate the suffering, and the suffering does not negate the peace/love. Perhaps this is similar to finding Nirvana and the Great Compassion in *samsara*—the world of suffering.

KS: Yes, this is the same in Zen. But I am interested in what Jesus said at the last moment on the Cross.

DM: He said, "Into your hands I commit my spirit."

KS: With the cry "Why" there is a duality in the fact of suffering. When Jesus's spirit is one with God, there is no more "Why," only what you call peace. It is peace in some sense, but ultimately with his surrender, he goes beyond words. In the process of Zen meditation, the Why is penetrated to its core, and the dualistic and relative disappear. The flower returns to spring beyond relative beings. In Emptiness, suffering no longer contradicts peace. We can receive suffering or pain as Emptiness at work. But I do not like to say "peace." This is also a dualistic term: peace and non-peace. One need not say anything—just go through it.

DM: In Jesus Forsaken, the peace of God is the suffering.

KS: These words are the expression of the inexpressible. This is why there is silence in our monastery. The monastery is like a fountainhead of pure spring water beyond all words. It is like the Trappist monastery where they have a vow of silence. Thomas Merton was supposed to come to visit me after Bangkok. But he died of electric shock from a faulty fan when he was taking a shower.

DM: My spiritual community is called a Focolare, which means "hearth" or "fireplace." Here "fire" is the Love that is the essence of God that burns away all that keeps us from being the family of humankind gathered around the hearth in the warmth of Love and Unity. This presence of Love and Unity in our midst is the fountainhead of our spiritual life.

KS: Focolare. This is very interesting. The Tang Dynasty Zen master Tozan said, "The Dharma (Truth) is like a huge flame of fire."

DM: Do you find this kind of hearth reality of unity among your monks?

KS: Yes. I think it is the same kind of thing. I used to say, "I am the person who lights the candles of others." Each person has a candle, but it may not be lit. The light is the same, and the candles may be long or short, large of small. The goal is to be a carrier of a lighted candle to light the candles of others. In the monastic community, we are united in this light coming from our candles.

DM: Those of us in the Focolare are called "Focolarini" or "bearers of fire." We try to carry the light of the hearth to others to realize the last prayer of Jesus: "May they all be one."

KS: Today, the world needs a person like you who not only knows his or her own religion, but also has the ability and sympathy to understand the other side, like Buddhism.

DM: I feel that you understand our side too.⁹

Dialogues in the Abe-Cobb Group

The Abe-Cobb Group first met at the 1984 Buddhist-Christian dialogue in Hawai'i. I joined the group the next year. I will share about just two of our dialogues. First is the dialogue when the Abe-Cobb Group met to discuss consumerism and the environment, which are still major issues today. John Cobb noted that that consumerism is itself like a religion. All religions promise happiness and a fulfilling and meaningful life. As a member of the consumerism religion, one believes that one should devote his or her life to working in order to own more things: a bigger house, a more expensive car, and more and more luxuries. A member believes that these are the things that bring happiness. It is in the pursuit of these kinds of things that a person can find a truly meaningful life. Happiness and fulfilment are always just around the corner.

Stephanie Kaza, a Buddhist, presented some statistics on how consumerism has an impact on the environment. She discussed how the high rates of consumption are producing environmental destruction as fast as, if not faster than the rising population. Since the middle of the eighteenth century, the per

---

9 This dialogue is excerpted from: "A Dialogue with Kobori Nanrei Sohaku," *Japanese Religions*, Vol. 20, No. 2 (1986), pp. 19–32.

capita consumption of energy, meat, and lumber has doubled. Take lumber, for example. More than half of the earth's forest cover is now gone, and the harvesting of the rest is speeding up. Twenty percent of U.S. lumber goes into making packing crates and pallets that are discarded after they are used. Logging roads in the United States are two-and-a-half times the length of our national highway system.

Sulak Sivaraksa, the famous Buddhist activist from Thailand, said that two-thirds of the Thai forests have been cut down to send wood to Japan where it is made into chipboard. Some Buddhists in Thailand have ordained trees as monks and put robes around them. The workers will not cut down such a tree since it is like killing a monk. He asked the question: "How can we act ethically, consume responsibly in this interconnected net of production and consumption?" The Buddhists and Christians agreed that the real incentives weaving this net are economic ones in ways that increase someone's profit. They agreed that this is where religions can begin to work together to see what is going on, and what can be done by those of us who hold that there are higher values than what supports the almighty dollar.

Masao Abe noted that suffering comes from three root causes: hate, greed, and delusion. Hate represents a pushing away of what one does not desire, and greed is a pulling to oneself what one does desire. The delusion is that getting the things one wants, and getting rid of things one does not want, brings happiness. Does consumerism deliver real happiness, or does it foster more greed that can never be satisfied? Does consumerism deliver freedom from what one hates, or an addiction to things one wants? As Buddhists and Christians, we agreed that our religions call us to a vision of the world and to a way of living based on love for others, compassion for those in need, and protection of the environment. That vision takes into consideration much more than our own pleasure. It opens us up to loving-kindness and compassion that brings true happiness for ourselves and others.

Christians shared that true happiness arises from a deeper union with God who is Love, which, in turn, brings us a deeper unity with others. This means a sensitivity to justice and charity, seeing ourselves as servants of God, loving our neighbors, and caring for the needy, while building his kingdom on Earth in ways that demand self-sacrifice. Buddhists shared that true happiness arises from correct insight into the suffering conditions of our lives and the world around us. This entails mindfulness of the factors that cause this suffering and compassionate responses to these conditions. The values of humility and generosity in living for the good of others, respecting the needs of all living beings, and making choices that bring freedom, purity, and healing to all are essential to true happiness.

The Buddhist scholars said that Christians need to gain a clearer vision of the interdependent nature of the universe as a remedy for our consumerist sickness. Christian scholars noted that Thomas Aquinas wrote, "God is innermost in each thing and most deeply inherent in all things" (*Summa*, I, Q VIII). I added that if God creates according to God's nature that is the Trinity, God's presence in each and all things means a Trinitarian presence in creation. A Trinitarian vision of the cosmos can bring us to a stronger realization that all persons and living beings are our brothers and sisters to be loved. Francis of Assisi had such a vision and view of how we should live in the light of that vision. My point was that living our spiritual insights together as Buddhists and Christians can build a dialogue of action for the good of humanity and our planet.

At another Abe-Cobb Group dialogue, Geshin Tokiwa gave a presentation. Shin'ichi Hisamatsu, his teacher, taught that Awakening is not just a Buddhist experience. It is a universal realization of our true self that can be attained by anyone. It involves "casting off" our ordinary way of living and discovering a new way of living that expresses our true selfhood. This way of being, way of living our daily life, is like our "original face" before we applied the makeup of ordinary living according to our culture. So, the question that Tokiwa raised is this: "What is this original way of living?" Tokiwa said that he feels that two persons who represent this luminous and liberating way of life in Buddhism and Christianity are Maya and Mary, the mothers of the Buddha and Jesus Christ.

In Buddhism, there is the notion of *Tathagata-garbha*. *Tathagata* is a title for the Buddha that means "thus come, and thus gone." The Buddha, Buddhists believe, is the person who has thus come into the world in the most profound way, has gained the most profound liberation from the world, and has thus gone to Nirvana. *Garbha* means "womb" or "embryo." In the simplest sense, the notion of the "womb of the *Tathagata*" in Buddhism means that we all are like a womb containing the embryo of our true self. For a Buddhist, this means one can give birth within ourselves to the luminous life of the Buddha.

Tokiwa said that this "conception" can take place when we are empty, like a womb, of the ordinary way of living that is so unenlightened and so unproductive of true contentment, wisdom, and love. When we begin to let go, to be empty of selfish attachments to things, and begin to live more selflessly for the good of others, then we begin to find the embryo of our original way of living. Our true Buddha-nature begins to manifest within us and within our way of being for others.

He said that Maya, as the mother of the Buddha, is the model for this way of true living. This idea is represented in the fact that some Buddhist texts claim that as Maya carried the Buddha, she was transformed by his presence within her. Influenced by the Buddha within, Maya is said to have claimed,

"Now there is nothing deficient about me. There is no hatred, greed, or even any delusion of mind. I am full of the inner peace that comes from the deepest meditation. And my mind is free from any kind of attachment."

In a similar way, Tokiwa said, by following the model of Maya and being empty of self and caring for others, a person can discover a treasure within, a treasure that makes one truly rich. Buddhist spirituality is a way to empty our selfishness and generate our loving original mode of being. Tokiwa noted that Buddhist spiritualty involves the conjunction of contemplation and compassion, of contemplative insight and compassionate action, that bring about the virtuous qualities of the Buddha that grew in and transformed Maya. Tokiwa concluded that Maya was not only a woman, the mother of the Buddha, the model for self-emptying/self-giving, but she also represents the "Womb of Great Compassion" (*Mahakaruna-garbha*). She embodies the boundless and compassionate womb of spiritual maternity that brings new life to those who seek it.

Tokiwa said he sees this spiritual maternity in Mary, especially at the foot of the Cross where she watched her son die, and where she embraced in herself the pain of the Cross out of love. Tokiwa said, "As a matter of fact, it is in St. Mary that I see the *pieta* that I also see what we Buddhists call the *Tathagata-garbha*." Tokiwa also sees Mary as a model for all of us in realizing spiritual maternity of "compassion" for others. "Mary is not only a specific person," he said. "But she also stands for all humankind. The very same humanity that experiences so much suffering in the world can also be mother to God. We can all be the womb through which God can again touch and care for the world around us."

I had known Geshin Tokiwa for many years in the dialogue, and alone with him, he said, "Mary represents the original way of being of all humanity, at once in agony and in peace. When humanity fully lives together this original way of peace in sharing the suffering of the world for the sake of transforming it by love, then the coming of God will be complete. In the meantime, we have Mary as a model."

Shortly after that conversation, Tokiwa had an amazing Christian experience of Love. On Sunday, those of us who were Catholic wanted a Mass. Hans Küng offered the Mass in a small room. A number of Buddhists joined us to watch. Hans chose to pass the plate with the hosts around the room. After the Mass, Hans came up to me and said that after Tokiwa took a host and ate it, not knowing that it was reserved for Christians, he cried. Hans asked me to talk to Tokiwa about his experience that led to tears. I could not believe that Tokiwa cried. He was a strong Rinzai Zen Buddhist who never shows any emotion. But, I did ask him while we were in the kitchen. He thought for a moment and then said, "The deepest experience possible of infinite love." This made me wonder if God gave him the gift of Jesus for what he shared about Mary.

The First Gethsemani Encounter

The first of three inter-monastic encounters requested by His Holiness the Dalai Lama was held in 1996 at the Abbey of Gethsemani, home of Thomas Merton.[10] We invited twenty-five Buddhist monastics and twenty-five Christian monastics.

---

10 See: Donald W. Mitchell and James Wiseman, O.S.B., eds., *The Gethsemani Encounter: A Dialogue on the Spiritual Life by Buddhist and Christian Monastics* (New York: Continuum, 1999); Donald W. Mitchell and James Wiseman, O.S.B., eds., *Transforming Suffering: Reflections on Finding Peace in Troubled Times* (New York: Doubleday, 2003); Donald W. Mitchell and William Skudlarek, O.S.B., eds., *Green Monasticism: A Buddhist-Catholic Response to an Environmental Calamity* (New York: Lantern Books, 2010).

Among the Buddhists were His Holiness the Dalai Lama and Maha Ghosananda, the Supreme Patriarch of Buddhism in Cambodia. There were also Zen masters from Korea, Taiwan, Japan, and the United States. On the Christian side were such notable people as Basil Pennington and David Steindl-Rast, as well as Bernardo Olivera, Abbot General of the Trappists from Rome. There were also Buddhist and Christian laypersons: John Borelli, Ewert Cousins, Diana Eck, Jeffrey Hopkins, and Judith Simmer-Brown.

We came together to talk about four topics: spiritual practice of prayer and meditation, growth in the spiritual life, spiritual guidance and community life, and how spirituality is related to social engagement. We gathered the first morning in the chapter room, the core room of the monastery, to begin the encounter, expecting the dialogue to follow the outline we had produced to guide the discussion. But right away, comments were made and questions were asked that took the discussion in unexpected and fascinating directions. At one point, I put my pen down and thought, *This is not going the way we had expected it to go. A dialogue with monks and nuns is not like a dialogue with academics. I have to let go of my expectations and just watch what happens. There is an "event" unfolding here that is beyond what we planned.*

In fact, at the end of the dialogue, Ewert Cousins said that it was like a spiritual treasure chest had been opened before us. We were all being invited to look together at the riches of our monastic traditions that have been collected for centuries, and at the extraordinary promise of this dialogical monastic spiritual journey of our times. For example, in the unstructured dynamic of the dialogue, Brother Kevin Hunt asked about the nature of the mind. This brought forth from this treasure chest luminous wisdom about the Buddhist practice of mental transformation. Later, a question about the Cross by Roshi Norman

Fischer inspired a deep conversation about God and suffering. In fact, at the second Gethsemani Encounter, Norman shared that the previous dialogue had led him to study the Jewish scriptures, which moved him to reconnect to his Jewish roots under the guidance of a rabbi.

There were many incredible moments in this dynamic conversation. But the one that was especially powerful came from the presentation by Dom Armand Veilleux. Armand was Procurator General of the Cistercian Order in Rome. He spoke about the Trappist monastic community of Our Lady of Atlas in Tibhirine, Algeria. It was the community of seven monks who had been beheaded recently by Muslim terrorists. It was a moving story. The community of monks was founded in 1938, and it survived the war of independence and the departure of most of the European people from Algeria. When the terrorism of the present time began to knock on the monastery door, the brothers decided to stay as a sign of hope and solidarity with the local Church and Muslim people of Algeria who were suffering under this reign of terror. The monks wanted to give testimony by being ready to lay down their lives out of love for their friends.

Armand made the point that contemplation is not just an isolated event, act, or peak experience—it is a way of life. A person of contemplation lives in such a way that, with the grace of God, he or she can see God in everything and everyone. More than this, he or she can see everything and everyone with God's eyes—the eyes of Love. Contemplation is being present to everything and everyone in this way of insightful compassion. It is an extraordinary gift from God

The final three years of the community, when they had faced death every day, brought the monks to a new and deeper level of community life—a life in which they began to see with the eyes of contemplation. One of the gifts of contemplation that Dom Christian de Cherge, the abbot of the community, received in this deeper life of prayerfulness was to see their Muslim friends as God sees them. Here is what he wrote in one of his letters given to Armand:

> This is what I shall be able to do if God wills. Immerse my gaze in that of the Father, and contemplate with him his children of Islam just as he sees them, all shining with the glory of Christ, the fruit of his Passion, and filled with the Gift of the Spirit, whose secret joy will always be to establish communion and to refashion this likeness, playfully delighting in the differences.

Armand went on to say that he believed that nothing ever written about interreligious dialogue has reached such a depth of insight. Dom Christian is saying two things. First, that when one contemplates with God's eyes the followers of Islam, or Buddhism, or Judaism, etc., one sees in them a "shining" beauty. One sees the redemptive glory of God brought about by the Passion of Christ that reaches all humankind. Second, Dom Christian is saying that as a fruit of Christ's Passion, God is joyfully establishing a secret communion with persons of other faiths. God takes "secret joy" in this hidden communion. In this communion, God refashions each person in the original likeness and image of God, which has been distorted by the conditions of ordinary life. This original luminous beauty is revealed and reformed by a God who is "playfully delighting in the differences" between the religions of humankind. This is the reality of God/Love.

I would add that Armand said that just a few months before the Gethsemani Encounter, he had traveled to Algeria to receive the remains of the monks of Atlas. This moved many Buddhists and Catholics to tears. Someone said, "Let's go visit the grave of Thomas Merton." We went to the gravesite where we stood together in silence.

There at Gethsemani, you could feel a deep communion between all of us. It seemed to arise at the moment we gathered together. Perhaps the contemplative life of the participants made us all open to this reality. I can say that we found that our communication had become communion. We joyfully found ourselves to be fellow pilgrims, loving brothers and sisters, united in some mysterious manner, in some secret communion with each other on a journey into a transformed life.

Then, there is Dom Christian's phrase about God "playing delightfully with the differences." For me, this was one of the deepest statements made in interreligious dialogue. Do we Christians ever think that God plays delightfully with the differences between Christianity and other religions? Or, do we think that God puts up with the differences, tolerates the differences, or even resents the differences? Let us say that we believe something about God, and another religion believes something different. Since we hold that God revealed what we believe, we could conclude that God must be displeased with the other religion. What Dom Christian is saying is that when there is a religion that believes differently than we believe, or practices something different from what we practice, then God can play with the differences so that those persons, so dear to Him, can be brought to heaven.[11]

---

[11] It may be helpful to note that there are three kinds of theology of religions in Christianity: exclusivism, inclusivism, and pluralism. The first claims that only baptized Christians can be saved. The third claims that each religion produces salvation by itself. The second, which is the official Catholic view, is that through the grace of God working in the hearts of all persons, persons of all religions can reach salvation: "And I, when I am lifted up from the earth, will draw all people to myself" (Jn 12: 32).

Venerable Maha Ghosananda also gave a talk. He had experienced the horrible killing fields in Cambodia and then established temples in each of the Cambodian refugee camps in Thailand. He was called the "Gandhi of Cambodia," and at the time of our encounter had led peace walks against land mines around Cambodia. His talk was short and to the point. He said that we are all part of one human family, whether we are Buddhists or Christians or Muslims. When we accept this fact, we can begin to sit down together and fashion a peace that will bring humankind to its fullest development. He then went on to share how he had helped to build peace even with the Khmer Rouge.

"Loving one's enemy," he said, "was taught by Buddha and Christ. It can contribute to a reconciling that brings peace. Retaliation and revenge only continue the cycle of violence." He cited how the Buddha himself walked onto a battlefield to stop a war. Buddhists and Christians must have the courage to leave their peaceful temples or churches and enter the modern world of violence and suffering: the refugee camps, the prisons, the ghettos, the places where people labor under injustice. At the end, Venerable Maha Ghosananada said, "We are our temple." We carry our spiritual treasure within ourselves. And today, we are being challenged to take that treasure, that Buddha or Christ, to those most in need of peace.

In response to a question, Venerable Maha Ghosananda was very clear that, for a Buddhist, the journey to peace begins with oneself. "The Buddha found peace in his own heart and then taught the way to peace to his first five disciples. Today, Buddhism has spread around the world. Now, we must enter the deepest part of our temple, ourselves, and find peace before we try to give it to others."

A personal example of this approach to peacemaking came out in Venerable Maha Ghosananda's answer to another question. This question was quite a surprise to all of us. A very well respected Rinzai Zen master from Japan, Eshin Nishimura, rose from his seat and took the microphone. He said that many years ago, he visited a Cambodian refugee camp on the Thailand border. Nishimura described the scene:

> It was a desolate place. People were standing around with nothing really to do or anywhere to go. But, in the middle of the camp was a small hut-like building that was used as a Buddhist temple. Sitting on the dirt floor was a lone monk practicing meditation. Now, I recognize that the lone monk was you! My question to you is this: "What did you do there where there was nothing to do?"

This is actually a famous Zen *koan*. Venerable Maha Ghosananda responded without hesitating: "I was seeking peace within myself, so I had something to give the others in the camp." Actually, Venerable Maha Ghosananda and his followers did a number of things in the camps. They went to the hospice tents to care for the dying, and to the hospital tents to care for the sick and wounded. This was the practice of loving-kindness, a virtue that they taught by example. Venerable Maha Ghosananda and his monks practiced loving-kindness, compassion, and sympathetic joy with equanimity, or peacefulness equally with all persons, friends and enemies. And they taught those in the camp to do so in order to overcome their anger and desire for revenge. This kept them from returning to the battlefields to kill more people.

I would add that when I first saw the Venerable Maha Ghosananda, I was taken aback by his appearance. He is small in stature, wearing simple robes and sandals. His face projected a deep inner peace, and his lips formed a slight smile. I saw him sitting next to His Holiness the Dalai Lama once, and the same elusive smile was on the face of His Holiness. But what was most striking about his appearance was his skin. It seemed to shine—his whole body seemed to be glowing. So much so, that I went over once and touched his bare shoulder to see what his skin felt like.

At one point in the dialogue, His Holiness the Dalai Lama gave a formal teaching on Nirvana. He began with addressing the question: What makes the attainment of Nirvana possible? There are two factors. First is that the nature of the mind is "clear light." Second is that all defilements of the mind that blind it to the truth are superficial and can be removed. It is these obstructive factors, not the nature of the mind, that produce ignorance. What are the obstructive factors? The scriptures list afflictive emotional and mental factors. An example of the latter, according to a text by the famous Buddhist philosopher, Nagarjuna (ca. 150–250 CE), is the obstructive view that all things exist as separate and discrete entities. This causes ignorance about oneself and the world in which we live. We are all interrelated, and if we see this interrelatedness without obstruction, we find loving-kindness and compassion for all.

So, what is this ignorance? It is a type of consciousness that does not know the truth about the actual mode of being of the objects of consciousness. Aryadeva (ca. 170–270 CE) wrote that due to this kind of consciousness, one cannot escape the cycle of existence. It covers up the nature of luminous knowing that is the true nature of the mind of clear light. Instead, it fosters negative afflictive emotional factors of consciousness that block our path to truth and liberation. With the mind of clear light free from the negative blocking factors of ignorance, we can see that all things do not exist on their own, but arise interdependently.

What then is Nirvana? Nirvana is the final nature of the mind of clear light that can be realized by being separated from the obstructive factors of the mind and from ignorance of the truth. This final nature of the mind always exists, and when it is free from defilements, that final nature of the mind is called Nirvana. So, the very foundation of Nirvana is always within us. A further distinction is found in a statement by Nagarjuna that *samsara* (the world of suffering) is Nirvana. This means that Nirvana is not just of the mind, but it is the true nature of all phenomena. From this point of view, cyclic existence should not be seen as bad and Nirvana as good. Rather, the nature of cyclic existence and the final nature of Nirvana are the same.

At the Gethsemani Encounter, Buddhists and Christians came together on their spiritual journeys to pause, to share time with one another, to just be present to each other and listen, learn, grieve, and rejoice. This was a true dialogue of the heart. What we see here are signs that point beyond the frontiers of our religions toward a future of universal brotherhood and sisterhood among humanity and including nature. When Pope John Paul II spoke at interfaith gatherings about us being fellow pilgrims journeying into the Truth, I believe that he was speaking under the same inspiration by the Holy Spirit that we felt at the Gethsemani Encounter.

One final memory that has remained with me. One day, I looked out the window of the chapter room, and there was a very old monk standing on the grass with a cane. He was leaning over with his hand outstretched, reaching toward a small flower growing in the grass. But he was not moving. He was completely still, bending over, arm outstretched, and his hand held still above the flower. I watched him for a long time but eventually needed to turn my attention back to the dialogue. Later, I again looked out the window. The old monk was gone, and the flower was still there.

Mt. Hiei

In 2006, I was back in Japan for a Buddhist-Christian Symposium in Osaka. It was co-hosted by the Rissho Kosei-kai and the Tendai School of Buddhism that had invited members of the Focolare to join them in dialogue. The Buddhists present represented a number of different schools of Japanese Buddhism. I was especially impressed with one person who is the Patriarch of the Hosso School that is a version of Yogacara Buddhism from India. It is one of the oldest of the Nara schools of Buddhism dating to the eighth century. He dressed in very colorful and ornate robes and was an imposing figure. I was told he is on TV in Japan and is a highly respected monk. At dinner one evening, I asked him a few questions about his thoughts concerning Buddhism in Japan. He was very concerned about Japanese businessmen who work from early morning to late at night. It seems that they have little contact with their children, and as a result, some youth are acting out their frustration by getting low grades in school or getting into trouble. This is the most powerful way to get back at their fathers since in all Japanese families, the most important thing for children to do is to succeed in school so they can get into a good university that is a doorway to a lifetime job at a top company. Also, to get into trouble brings shame on the family.

His experience was shared by the other Buddhist leaders in the dialogue, and much of our discussion had to do with ethical and spiritual formation in the family. All the Japanese Rissho Kosei-kai, Tendai, and Focolare participants discussed how they are trying to address these topics from their religious points of view. These dialogical goals had been discussed at meetings of the Focolare and the Rissho Kosei-kai in the recent past.

While this was the main focus of the dialogue, one monk from the sacred Mt. Hiei of the Tendai School shared a kind of practice on the mountain that goes back centuries. Mt. Hiei is the most famous religious mountain in Japan. It was there that the founders of Soto Zen, Pure Land Buddhism, and Nichiren Buddhism were trained in their early years. The Tendai monk shared about how he had to run from one site on the mountain to another for days on end with very little sleep, food, or water until he had a vision that showed him what path he was to take in his Tendai training. In fact, one aspect of Tendai is esoteric about which I knew nothing. So, I found his talk very interesting . . . and, in a way, it prepared me for my visit to Mt. Hiei.

At the end of the dialogue, we were all in a bus passing through truly beautiful countryside on our way to visit Mt. Hiei. As we climbed up the mountain, we could see down to a pristine lake with pine trees surrounding it. Also, it was cherry blossom season. To tell the truth, I could not appreciate what that meant until I saw it for myself. There are cherry trees everywhere along the road, and when the wind blew, the blossoms filled the air and covered the ground like snowflakes. A number of times, our bus seemed to be showered by white blossoms.

We arrived at the new guest house in the early evening. Before dinner, I took a walk by myself to see some of the nearby temples and other religious sites up and down the mountainside. The trees were gigantic and ancient. The monastic complex dates back to the ninth century. Going up the mountain, there were some small temples, and then to the left, I saw one of the major temples that dates back to the founding of the monastic complex. It is famous for having three oil lamps that have burned uninterrupted for 1,200 years. Since it was closed for the night, I circled it, and as I did so, I felt a deep joy.

Then, I returned to the guest house for dinner. Afterwards, a monk told us about the history of Mt. Hiei and explained that the next morning, we would go to the temple I had seen for a special morning service. He suggested that we close our eyes and go inside ourselves during the service and see what happens. He said that the ritual can induce visions. This reminded me of the Tendai monk who had talked about his vision on the mountain.

The next morning, we were taken to a wooden platform in front of the temple where we were invited to sit for the ceremony. Near where we sat, there were some low windows. We could see that in the room inside, there was a huge space that was filled with ancient religious items. In front of an altar, there were the three oil lamps burning. Also, we could hear monks chanting.

At one point, a very elderly monk was brought onto the platform right in front of us. He was carried there by other monks who placed him onto a seat where he began to chant and hit a wooden hammer against a hollow wooden block. The sound was strong and clear in the morning silence. I asked the monk next to me about his age since he seemed very old. He was 104. "But," the monk said, "he is the younger leader. The elder leader of the monastery is 112. He does not leave his house but gives lessons each morning to the novices." I thought to myself that living on this mountain with healthy food, plenty of exercise, and quiet meditation would certainly make for a long life.

Remembering what the monk had suggested the night before, I closed my eyes. With each sound from the wooden block, I seemed to descend deeper and deeper down a hole in the ground. Soon, it seemed like I was descending faster and faster, and I became afraid. I prayed to Jesus. Each time I said "Jesus," the descent stopped, and from around the platform I was on appeared small persons with white cloths around their waists. They were below me and knelt in deep silent adoration. I remembered Paul writing that "At the name of Jesus the

Lord, every knee will bend, in heaven and on earth and under the earth" (Philippians 2:10). After a moment of devotion, the little persons disappeared behind the platform, and the descent continued.

Finally, we reached what seemed like a flat ground that extended limitlessly. On the ground was a man who was heavy-set, bearded, and dancing with a stoic face. He would jump up and kick out one leg and then drop down, jump up again, and kick out the other leg. He seemed like an old Jewish man dancing a traditional dance. He did that over and over. As I watched him, I asked myself, "But what is this about?" The man stopped, stood still, and looked at me. Then, he began to dance again. I asked this question three times, and each time, he stopped and looked at me. Suddenly, the ceremony ended and I opened my eyes. I was back sitting on the platform.

Years later, I was at a Buddhist-Christian dialogue of the Focolare in Italy. One of the Buddhist leaders was a leading Tendai monk from Mt. Hiei. I asked him about my experience during that ceremony. As I told him the story, he would nod and say, "Yes, that is right." He seemed to know what I was experiencing and that it was common. But, when I mentioned the dancing man, he said that part was for me and only I could explain it. He said, "Mt. Hiei is populated with spirits of the departed who are attached to this world and remain here. They are dressed as you describe them, and we have built spirit houses around the mountain for them to live in as an act of kindness to them." I knew about what in Buddhism are called "hungry ghosts" since they are hungry for this world and not ready to move on. After the monk said that the dancing man was for me alone, I thought about my best friend who was Jewish, overweight, and had a beard. He had died suddenly a few years earlier after my visit to Mt. Hiei.

Masao Abe

Through the Abe-Cobb Group, I got to know Masao Abe well, and we became good friends. He was born in 1915 in Osaka to a family of six children. Early on, he was raised a Pure Land Buddhist and had a strong devotion to Amida Buddha. In 1942, just a few months after the Japanese attack on Pearl Harbor, he entered Kyoto University. Shin'ichi Hisamatsu was then a professor at Kyoto University, and Abe was attracted to him even though Hisamatsu was a Zen Buddhist. Abe, like many of the other students, were attracted to Hisamatsu given his spiritual depth in the midst of the war since the students were all against the war. Abe and other students created a Buddhist Youth Organization at Kyoto University under Hisamatsu's guidance. This group later became the FAS Society.

Abe's conversion to Zen was difficult. Once during a retreat with Hisamatsu in 1951, he jumped up from his cushion and rushed Hisamatsu, grabbing him. Abe looked at Hisamatsu's face and asked him, "Is that the true self?"

Hisamatsu solemnly replied, "That is the true self."

Abe said, "Thank you" and left the room.

In the evening Abe again approached Hisamatsu and tapped him on the head. Hisamatsu said, "Is that all you can do? Do more!" Abe slapped him with all his might, but Hisamatsu calmly laughed. Abe ran out of the building into the cold winter and jumped into a well full of ice water. At a later retreat, Abe had a private meeting with Hisamatsu.

Abe said, "I just cannot find any place where I can stand."

Hisamatsu said, "Stand right at that place where there is nowhere to stand." Abe eventually attained Awakening after this great struggle. When Hisamatsu was dying, Abe made a personal vow to his teacher to dedicate his life to presenting Zen to the West.

In 1990, Abe's primary text on God and Emptiness was published in *The Emptying God: A Buddhist-Jewish-Christian Conversation*.[12] He sent a pre-publication copy for me to use in writing my book, *Spirituality and Emptiness: The Dynamics of Spiritual Life in Buddhism and Christianity*.[13] In my own book, I discussed different views about Emptiness in the Kyoto School and *kenosis* in Christian spirituality. Based on this collaboration, I received a grant to bring Abe and his wife Ikuko to my university for two years. When Abe and his wife came to Purdue University in 1992, I came to know his spiritual depth, gentle compassion, and great intellect.

During those two years, we developed a collaboration. Also, the grant enabled me to host four dialogues around the state of Indiana. The first one was with Marjorie Suchocki on the theme of "peace." Abe described peace as living the Great Compassion at the center of one's being. Suchocki responded with a Trinitarian view of "unity in diversity" that supports peace. The second dialogue was with Wolfhart Pannenberg on Abe's notion of a "kenotic God." Pannenberg saw *kenosis* as just the action of the Son out of obedience of the will of the Father. Abe responded that if Christ is the self-revelation of God, then the *kenosis* of Christ is revelatory of the very nature of God as Love.

The third dialogue was with Richard Rubenstein on "The Holocaust, God, and Evil." Rubenstein stressed the need for clarification of the causes of the Holocaust through the academic studies of psychology, the social and political sciences, and history and economics. Abe declared that until humanity

---

12 John Cobb and Christopher Ives, eds., *The Emptying God: A Buddhist-Jewish-Christian Conversation* (New York: Orbis Books, 1990).

13 Donald W. Mitchell, *Spirituality and Emptiness: The Dynamics of the Spiritual Life in Buddhism and Christianity* (New York: Paulist Press, 1991).

faces ignorance and the "blind will" of human nature, there will always be evil in the world. When people are blinded by their ignorance, their will is moved by anger, frustration, and other factors that lead to violence against the "other." Only when humanity finds a compassionate center within, and the interrelatedness of the world around them, can such evil come to an end.

Finally, the fourth dialogue was with Keith J. Egan on the theme of meditation. Egan traced the historical development of various forms of meditation in the Church. He emphasized that in Christianity, there is a difference between meditation and contemplation. The latter is caused by the grace of God. Abe replied that in Buddhism, meditation culminates in wisdom by a process where one realizes he or she cannot achieve wisdom by his or her own will. While this realization is found in Christianity as well, in Buddhism, awakening is not achieved by grace that results in union with God. It is achieved by the true self awakening to itself. Egan noted that in Christianity, there is also an overcoming of unhealthy attachments and the false self.

During his time at Purdue, we had many conversations about the experiential basis for our views. Abe and I discussed the words of Pseudo-Dionysius: "dazzling darkness." For Abe, this meant that Nirvana is totally identified with the world of *samsaric* darkness. He would say that the Godhead of infinite light and love must be seen in all of creation. The *kenosis* of the Godhead in creation affirms that it is full of Love and Light. Abe found this same *kenosis* in the Trinity that defines the relationality of the Trinity as total self-giving Love. My response was that the two are different. The experience of the *kenosis* in the Trinity as a Love and Light is different from the *kenosis* of creation as well as the *kenosis* incarnate in Jesus Christ. Von Balthasar refers to the *ur-kenosis* of Love in the Trinity that is the foundation of the other two—in creation and in Jesus. And he claims that the *ur-kenosis* of the Trinity is the foundation of eternal life in Paradise.[14]

After a year or so, our discussions changed. He knew of the similarities between the spirituality of the FAS Society founded by Hisamatsu during World War II, and the Focolare that was also founded during World War II by Chiara Lubich. He had read some of the writings of Lubich and liked them very much. In 1992, he and his wife visited Luminosa, the retreat center for the Focolare in Hyde Park, New York, where he received the Luminosa Prize for his work in dialogue. He and Ikuko were taken by the communal spirit of the community that was similar to that of FAS. At one point, Abe was asked to plant a small tree in the peace garden. He said that he would like to put a stone in the garden. When asked why, he said, "In a garden, the flowers are like words, and stones are the silence between the words."

At his request, I helped plan for he and Ikuko to go to Rome to meet with Chiara Lubich and Pope John Paul II. Abe asked if he could also meet with Cardinal Joseph Ratzinger because he was having difficulty understanding the official Catholic position on different issues as he talked to a range of Catholic theologians in the United States. So, in March of 1993, Abe and his wife went to Rome. Unfortunately, Chiara Lubich was ill and undergoing treatment in Switzerland, and Cardinal Ratzinger was in Asia. But the couple was hosted at the Focolare Center in Rome where Masao Abe talked to members of the Abba School. It is made up of theologians and other scholars who study the unpublished mystical writings of Chiara Lubich. Members of the Focolare took them on a tour of Rome, Assisi, Florence, and Loppiano.

---

14 Has Urs von Balthasar, *Theo-Logic II: Truth of God* (San Francisco: Ignatius Press, 2004). p. 97.

Then, they went to the Congregation for the Doctrine of the Faith of which Cardinal Ratzinger was president. Abe met for a long discussion with Fr. Jacues Servais, S.J., and Fr. Piero Coda, who is also a member of the Abba School. At the end of the meeting, Cardinal Ratzinger entered the room. He had returned to Rome earlier than expected. Cardinal Ratzinger said he had been in Hong Kong and wanted to come right away on his return to tell Abe that he felt that his work had historical significance. So, Servais and Coda confirmed teachings of the Church for Abe, and Ratzinger confirmed the importance of Abe's work.

The next day, the Fr. John Masayuki Shirieda, Under Secretary of the Secretariat for Non-Christians, and Enzo Fondi, from the Focolare's Center for Interreligious Dialogue, took the Abes to meet the Pope. Pope John Paul II greeted Masao Abe and encouraged him as a "fellow pilgrim" to continue his work and his "spiritual journey into the Truth." He thanked Abe for his work in the dialogue. When the Pope turned to Ikuko Abe, she told him that his presence gave her hope. He looked into her eyes and said, "Let us carry the Cross together." Upon their return, both Masao and Ikuko said to me that at that moment, the Pope entered the deepest part of their being.

CHAPTER 3

Pope John Paul II and the Vatican's First Dialogues with Buddhism

In 1986, I was on sabbatical with my family living outside of Rome near the Focolare Center for Interreligious Dialogue. One of the directors, Fr. Enzo Fondi, encouraged me to meet Fr. Marcello Zago, OMI, the Secretary at the Secretariat for Non-Christians (SNC). Marcello had lived in Laos for twenty years, including during the Vietnam War. I went into Rome to hear him give a talk at a Buddhist Center, and I was very impressed by his talk and with him as a person. Also, one of his pant legs had a torn area that he had stitched by hand. This is not what you see in the Vatican! So, I asked if I could meet with him. It turned out that the OMI Center was near where we were living. He and I met several times to talk about the Church's interreligious dialogues and also the Church's theology of religions. In the end, he asked if I agreed in my heart with the Church's approach to interreligious dialogue in particular, and to other religions in general. I could honestly say that I did. "Then," he replied, "you can help us with the Buddhists."

He invited me to the Vatican's offices for the SND where he introduced me to Cardinal Arinze, president of the SND, and to Under Secretary Fr. John Masayuki Shirieda, SDB, who was responsible for Asia. We had a long talk. At the end, Cardinal Arinze asked me to be their consultant on Buddhism. Then, Fr. Shirieda took me into his office, and we had a personal conversation. He knew about my lectures in Japan where he was born and raised. John said that as a youth he lived in a village in Japan. There was an orphanage in his village run by a Catholic priest. One night, the orphanage caught on fire. The priest kept running back into the building to bring out children. No one else tried to help him. In the end, the priest died. John was so impressed that he took an oath to become a priest to replace the priest who had died. He did and eventually found his way to the office of the SNC. Over time, I gained a great respect for Cardinal Arinze, Fr. Marcello Zago, and Fr. Shirieda. They had come to the Vatican from Nigeria, Laos, and Japan to lead the Church's dialogues with other religions.

The Vatican's First Dialogue with Buddhism: Taiwan

A number of Catholic and Buddhist scholars, including myself, went to the monastery of the Fo Guang Shan Buddhist Order in Kaohsiung, Taiwan in 1995 to address something that happened six months prior. That was when Pope John Paul II published *Crossing the Threshold of Hope*,[1] which had a chapter dedicated to Buddhism. Buddhist leaders and scholars around the world took exception to some statements that were written in that chapter. Then, a few months after the publication of the book, the Pope visited Sri Lanka. He was to meet with the

---

1 Pope John Paul II, *Crossing the Threshold of Hope* (New York: Alfred A. Knopf, 1994).

Buddhist leadership, but they boycotted the meeting. Soon after the Pope's visit to Sri Lanka, there was a desire to hold a world dialogue not to address the book, but issues raised by the book.

Cardinal Arinze organized this dialogue in Taiwan and invited ten Buddhist representatives from Sri Lanka, Thailand, Taiwan, Tibet, Japan, and the United States. He also invited ten Catholic representatives from Europe, Asia, and the United States. I was the representative from the United States. I chose Robert Aitken Roshi to join me as the United States Buddhist representative. Cardinal Arinze brought three other representatives from the Pontifical Council for Interreligious Dialogue (PCID) that replaced the Secretariat for Non-Christians under Pope John Paul II.

It is important to note that we came to this dialogue not to discuss the Pope's book or the boycott, but in order to reach a mutual understanding concerning certain topics in question. This gave us a framework in which to clarify the teachings of both of our traditions. There were four areas of discussion. First was the point of departure in the religious journey, namely, the human condition and the need of liberation. Second was the point of arrival of the religious journey, namely, what we consider ultimate reality. For Christians, that means God; for Buddhists, it means Nirvana or Buddhahood. Third, we discussed the roles of Christ and Buddha in these spiritual journeys. Finally, we discussed the role of personal practice and social engagement in the journey.

I arrived in Taiwan in the middle of Typhoon Gary. On the night we arrived, we all entered a large lecture hall with thousands of Buddhists waiting for us, despite the typhoon. We sat in the front row. On stage was Cardinal Arinze, the Venerable Master Hsin Ting from Fo Guang Shan, Archbishop Joseph Ti-kang of Taipei, and the Secretary of State of Taiwan. Personally, I was exhausted due to traveling in the typhoon, being hungry, and feeling uncomfortable with thousands of persons looking at us. Then, I had another Buddhist esoteric experience. A Buddha statue on the stage in front of me caught my attention, and I heard, "The self you are worried about does not exist." Suddenly, I experienced all the anxiety "flying" out of the left side of my head. I was relaxed and happy. In Buddhism, this is called "a worldly benefit." After the program, we went into a private room for a wonderful dinner followed by a short gathering where instructions were given. Finally, I presented, "Status Questions: Taking Stock of the Present Buddhist-Christian Dialogue."

The next morning, the dialogue began. Each day, we met as a group to listen to presentations and to dialogue through questions and answers. We began with a moment of silence, followed by the presentations that were intended to stimulate ensuing dialogue. In the evenings, we met in small groups where we could go in depth about issues raised in the larger group. I found these small group discussions to be very valuable. I felt much more comfortable asking questions and entering the give and take of dialogue with a small group of people whom I came to know and trust. Trust is so important in any relationship, especially when you open up and share from the heart. I must add here that the wonderful hospitality of the Fo Guang Shan Monastery contributed greatly to the warm atmosphere of our meeting, and thus to the success of our encounter.

On a personal note, one day when Bob Aitken and I were walking together, I shared with him my experience of hearing the scraping of the banana leaf on the window screen during my final *zazen* practice at his *Zendo*. He stopped walking and said, "That is the experience of the Pure Land. The Pure Land shines in all things since each thing contains the whole universe." That was interesting to me because the Japanese view of the Pure Land is that it is the celestial realm of Amida Buddha where one can go after death through the grace of Amida. But then, I remembered that in the original Chinese school of Pure Land Buddhism, there are two views. One is focused on being reborn in the Pure Land through faith. The other is focused on experiencing the Pure Land here as the hidden reality of this world. The latter is what Bob was talking about. It was also interesting to be at Fo Guang Shan because they are teaching another view of the Pure Land based on what is called today Humanistic Buddhism. The goal of Fo Guang Shan is to create a Pure Land by social engagement to end poverty and other social and environmental ills.

Also, the beauty of Fo Guang Shan was a joy to the senses, both physically and spiritually. You feel you are in a Pure Land. The new Dharma Hall and the huge Buddha Hall give one a sense of spiritual grandeur. The grounds with traditional Chinese landscaping is a real source of peacefulness and recollection. The sincere practice of the monks and nuns gave the monastic complex an atmosphere that is both uplifting and spiritual. At that time, there were eight hundred nuns and two hundred monks in training. Also, our hosts graciously provided the Catholics with a beautiful room for daily Mass and private adoration of the Eucharist. The moments celebrating Mass with Cardinal Arinze and the Taiwan bishops in a Buddhist monastery were deeply moving experiences for me. It was as if you could feel the presence of Jesus among us.

At the end of our dialogue, I was the leader of the drafting committee that composed a "Final Statement." I must say that we felt a lot of pressure as we worked late into the night, given the tense situation between the Church and the Buddhist world. On one hand, we knew that PCID would be taking the statement back to the Vatican where it would be read by the Pope and Cardinal Ratzinger. On the other hand, we were aware that our Buddhist members also needed an official statement that they could show their own leaderships.

The final morning, Professor Nara, president of Komazawa University in Japan, and I presented our work to the full encounter group. I was to do this alone, but I suggested a strong Buddhist leader join me. To our delight, there were only a few minor changes suggested, and the "Final Statement" with these changes was unanimously approved. It was then made clear by the Catholic leadership that this document will be the reference point for the Church's future dialogues with Buddhism. And, all of our Buddhist participants felt that this was a document they could take home with no reservations. The following is a summary of the statement.

First, the statement rejects the view that Buddhism has a negative view of the world as the cause of all sufferings. Rather, "The traditional Buddhist analysis posits karmic energy rooted in ignorance and selfish attachment as the cause of human suffering and evil. Buddhists propose a path of high morality, deep meditation practice, and profound wisdom as the antidote to this condition." The statement also makes it clear that Christianity affirms our human limitations not only come from our creaturely status, but also as a consequence of original sin. This legacy "produces the limitations of ignorance, concupiscence, alienation from self, others, and God." It also states that it is through the Paschal Mystery of the passion, death and resurrection of Jesus Christ that "the human condition is definitively transformed through participation in the divine life of grace."

Second, the statement affirms that while Buddhism is not a form of theism, it does not deny the existence of God. Rather, Buddhism focuses on "a subtle, selfless, pure, and unattached balance between awakened wisdom and compassionate engagement with the world . . . both selfless liberation and the freedom to live fully for the good of others." The statement says that for Christians, the ideal "is always viewed in a theistic perspective. As pilgrims on earth, Christians are called to find perfection in union with God . . . a dynamic and communal participation in the life of the Trinitarian God. Since God is light and love, this perfection entails both love of God and love of neighbor. This life of love is nourished by the word of God and the sacraments."

Third, the statement affirms that Buddhism does not have a "negative soteriology" that leads to the rejection of our humanity. Rather, "Buddhahood or Nirvana that can be achieved are positive conditions of human wholeness and freedom characterized by loving-kindness, compassion, sympathetic joy, and equanimity of affinity, so that one can live fully for the good of others." The statement also affirms that Christians receive grace flowing from Jesus Christ: "In Jesus Christ, we see the infinite love of God as a fountainhead of salvation. In Jesus Christ, we can also find the positive fulfillment of our existence, our happiness in God, and loving care for the benefit of others as well."

Fourth, the statement affirms that Buddhism does not focus on detachment from the problems of the world. Rather, Buddhists state that "by applying the teachings of the Buddha to their personal and social circumstances, [Buddhists] engage in forms of social service and spiritual service." This kind of effort to address social and spiritual ills is also stressed on the Christian side: "It is the detachment taught by Jesus Christ that makes one free to actualize the liberation won for us by him. . . . This social dimension of liberation calls the Christian to dedicate himself or herself consciously and totally toward a life of charity and service to other persons, with a preferential option for the poor, and develops a particular sensitivity to the global environment."

The conclusion of the "Final Statement" says that:

> Buddhists and Christians are all quite aware that we are gathering in a world "torn by division and strife, poverty and injustice, violence and war." We also recognize

that there is a worldwide erosion of spiritual and moral values, and also the destruction of nature. We affirm the need for all religions to promote personal and social transformation to contribute to a more united and peaceful world. We find that interfaith dialogue on the frontiers of our traditions can itself be a prophetic call to our religious brothers and sisters to work together for this goal. Interfaith friendships can be signs of hope, inspiring us to seek a universal spiritual foundation for a greater unity among all peoples and nations.

The Vatican's Second Dialogue with Buddhism: India

At the first dialogue in Taiwan, Buddhists requested more dialogues with the Vatican. Therefore, a second encounter took place in India in 1998. Ann went with me, and when we arrived at the Bombay airport after midnight, Lalitha Krishna, a well-known Hindu leader, had arranged for a van to take us to a local hotel. In the morning, we met Roberto Catalano, who was responsible for the Focolare in India, and he accompanied us to Bangalore. I had been to many places in the world, but this was the biggest culture shock I ever experienced. The smells, colors, shapes, and sounds as well as the people and animals overwhelmed my senses. For example, on the main street, cows walked around, bullock carts were given the right of way, auto-rickshaws and motor scooters were zipping by, beggars were sitting on the curbs, and groups of women were breaking tiles and rocks with small tools to make new sidewalks. The stores we passed were a mix of new and ancient. It seemed to me that the modern world was placed on top of the ancient world everywhere you looked. And at the same time, I felt drawn into this new world with a fascination for what seemed like a kind of hidden dimension within and below it all.

In Bangalore, Roberto took us to see the Hindu religious sites. We saw, among other things, the Bull Temple and the Ramakrishna Mission. Walking around the statue of Nandi the Bull, I could almost sense his breathing—like he was alive. This enlivenment of certain statues is a belief in Hinduism. The Ramakrishna Order serves a meal to the lepers of Bangalore each day. They have an interesting system. If a donor gives a certain amount of money, not much by our standards, they can use it to feed all the lepers in and around the city for one day. They name that day after the donor. So, there was an Ann and Don Mitchell day.

We traveled from Bangalore to the conference site at the Asirvanam Benedictine Monastery in the jungle off the road to Madras. Along the route, we saw something on the edge of the city that affected our lives forever. It is called a "hutment." It stretches for what seems like miles. It is made up of small huts made out of palm branches. They are only about five feet high and maybe ten feet wide. The sides are open, and in the middle of the huts is a dug-out area where there can be a fire. Around the sides of the huts are some belongings. People sit and sleep on the ground. The huts are close together, and women weave between them with plastic pots on their heads going for food and water.

We eventually arrived in the Asirvanam monastery for the dialogue. It is situated in the jungle near a small village. The village life seemed quite simple and pleasant. The monastery had a banana plantation and employed men from the village. Also, there was work being done on the grounds by women from the village. There was also a small school run by the monastery with about two dozen children attending daily.

When we first arrived, the rooms in the new guesthouse were not finished, so we stayed the first night in the old guesthouse. Each small room had whitewashed walls and a clay floor. Two beds were against the sidewalls made of wood planks with mats on them with mosquito nets. The doorway in the back of the room led to a lean-to behind the room with branches for a roof. It was the bathroom area. For the shower, there was a waist-high waterspout. You sat on a plastic stool and ran the water into a large bucket. Then, you dipped a small bucket into the water and poured it over you, causing the clay floor to become muddy. At night, we could hear monkeys on the roof and jackals howling nearby. We were also warned of cobras coming into our room. If one bit us, we were to go to the monastery and push a red button near the door, and someone would come out and give us a shot to save our lives. As we went to bed and listened to the jackals in the jungle and the monkeys on the roof, I said to Ann, "Well, Ann, we are not in Kansas anymore!"

The next day, we moved to our new quarters. However, Professor Nara, who was in the room next to ours, said that a cobra had come into his room, and he was flying back to Japan. Actually, the name of the place where the monastery is located is called the "Field of Vipers." I asked if there were other snakes besides cobras and was told that the cobras killed them all. Fortunately, our new quarters were quite comfortable by comparison. There was one issue, however. A monk told us that we did not need mosquito netting, but during the first night, I could hear mosquitos in the room. When I looked at the only window in the room, I saw that the screen was not tightly set in the window frame, and I could not make it fit. So, I sprayed some mosquito repellent around the window, hitting some mosquitos in the process. Then, I asked one of the monks to please give us some mosquito netting, which he did.

That morning in the conference room of the monastery, we had our first dialogue. We were sitting in a circle at student desks. I was reading along with the person who was presenting his paper when a really huge mosquito flew over my shoulder and landed on the paper I was reading. It was truly the biggest mosquito I have ever seen! It turned around on the paper and faced me. It was at least ten o'clock in the morning, way past the time mosquitos are out. As I sat looking at it, the Venerable U. Panna Dipa from Myanmar, who was sitting next to me, leaned over and said, "Big mosquito!" I nodded. He then took a piece of paper and waved it in the air, blowing the mosquito away. I thought that this may have been the "mother of all mosquitos" coming to ask me: "Why did you kill my children?" Only in India would I think of this. In any case, I promised at that moment not to kill any living being again. I remembered my first audience with His Holiness the Dalai Lama when he talked about the precept of non-harming of all living beings. I have kept my promise to this day.

As time passed, Ann and I began to get accustomed to this new world and relaxed and enjoyed our surroundings. There was a very tall and broad tree in the jungle that had bright red flowers covering its branches. Below it were anthills that were at least four feet tall. In the mornings, little children ran to school laughing and yelling at each other. In the afternoons, young girls with beautiful flowers in their hair sang joyful songs as they worked outside the monastery. The village was poor, but the people were happy and had a sense of dignity. Once, we walked the dirt path from the monastery to the banana plantation. There was a swarm of bees or wasps overhead that was the size of a cloud, but it passed without a hint of danger.

One day, a group of about twelve young Indian Catholic monks were packing up their things and putting them into an old school bus. I asked them what they were doing. "We are going to make a new monastic foundation deeper in the jungle," one young monk said. I had to marvel at their courage, commitment, and faith. I looked at what was being put in the bus. There were some plastic buckets, mats for sleeping, very few pieces of clothing, and some personal items. That was all.

"Where will you stay?" I asked.

"God will provide," was the answer. "We will sleep under the trees at first, and then see what God has in mind for us. Right now, we are putting ourselves into His hands, to serve Him by being one with the people we serve."

This was the kind of spirit that the organizers of this dialogue wanted our Buddhist friends from Asia to see. This was the new Church in Asia: making itself one with the poor and the marginalized, living as they do, and providing what they can for those most in need. Here is a silent monastic witness to the words of Christ. These monks lived like the villagers, and then like the people deeper in the jungle. When we attended Mass, we saw a joyful celebration in a simple church fully enculturated with songs, drums, dances, dress, flowers, incense, and fire like you see in a Hindu temple. The Mass was deeply moving and seemed to have no boundaries, opening to infinity.

As for the dialogue itself, there were eighteen of us participating in a discussion of the theme: "Word and Silence in Buddhism and Christianity." The evening before our formal meetings, we began with a welcoming program that included the traditional Indian lighting of a lamp, readings from Christian and Buddhist scriptures, a moment of prayerful silence, and a performance of an Indian sacred dance by one of the young Benedictine monks. In his opening remarks, Cardinal Arinze said that in our modern world so full of noise, people seem to be afraid of silence lest they feel obliged to change their lives and attend to deeper realities than what is found in our secular societies. We need to see the importance of silence, he noted, and turn our attention to what is truly holy in life.

The dialogue addressed four topics: "Buddhist Enlightenment and Christian Revelation," "Sacred Texts in the Buddhist and Christian Traditions," "Meditation and Contemplation in Buddhism and Christianity," and "*Anatta-Sunyata* and *Kenosis*." Papers were presented for four days that stimulated a free exchange among all of us in general sessions. As in Taiwan, we also met in very fruitful small group sessions, where we could pursue issues raised in the larger group in more depth. The following are summaries of our discussions of these topics.

In terms of the first three topics, in Buddhism, *scripture* is a guide for living, and the texts used in the recitation of scripture. They are a powerful tool for both mental and moral cultivation. Today, there are many lay movements in Buddhism that use such recitation to help their members live the teachings of the Buddha in daily life. Also, silent meditation deepens wisdom insight into the truths taught in the scriptures. Silence provides a spiritual environment in which purification and growth can take place, leading to enlightenment. Enlightenment is not just knowledge; it is the transforming wisdom that brings the ultimate freedom of Nirvana or Buddhahood, characterized by compassion, loving-kindness, sympathetic joy, and equanimity reflected in one's thoughts, words, and actions.

In Christianity, scripture is also a guide for instruction and formation. The Word of God is used in community worship and celebration, in both formal liturgy and informal sharing. Christians believe that the Word of God is a revelation that carries the power to transform one's life in accord with the mind and heart of Christ, the Word of God. One is nourished by the word of God in prayer and meditation. A traditional practice of meditation on the scriptures is *lectio divina,* or sacred reading, that guides one through reading scripture, meditation on scripture, personal response in prayer, and silent contemplation that is given one by God's grace. The effect of deep silence, prayer, and contemplation leads to an ever-deeper experience of God's presence, one's true self, and a renewed life dedicated to social transformation. In Christianity, one also looks for guidance in the words of the Fathers of the Church, the great saints, as well as personal guidance in spiritual direction.

At our fourth dialogue on Emptiness and *kenosis*, Geshe Damdul Namgyal of the Tibetan tradition gave a profound talk about Emptiness. For him, following an important school of Mahayana Buddhism, Emptiness is ultimate reality. In the experience of Emptiness, one finds that the things of the world are "empty" of the independent existence we perceive. Rather, all things exist interdependently; everything is what it is due to a hidden interconnectedness that is itself compassion. Geshe said, "The failure to see this Emptiness of interrelatedness prevents compassion. Until we can realize the Emptiness of ourselves as our interrelatedness with others, compassion in the purest sense cannot grow." Geshe described how the realization of the lack of independent selfhood places one in the deeper interconnectedness of life, free and compassionate, and able to dedicate oneself to the service of others.

My talk on *kenosis* was based on Paul's *Letter to the Philippians* (2:5–8) where he wrote that we should have:

> The same attitude that is also yours in Christ Jesus, who though he was in the form of God, did not regard equality with God something to be grasped. Rather, he *emptied* himself, taking the form of a servant, coming in human likeness; and found human in appearance, he humbled himself, becoming obedient to death, even death on a cross. (2:5–8)

For John of the Cross, this emptying, or *kenosis,* comes from God's grace. John says that "nobody is able to empty himself of all his appetites to reach God" (*Ascent*, 1:1, 5). It is God who pours his luminous love into the spiritual depths of a person as a "fire" that consumes all that needs healing in one's life. For John, this spiritual emptying and the resulting union with God reveals a new vision of the cosmos: "It seems . . . that the entire universe is a sea of love in which it is engulfed, and one becomes conscious of the living point or center of love within itself, and one is unable to catch sight of the boundaries of this love" (*The Living Flame of Love*, 2:10).

As we came to understand the similarities and differences of our religions, we were able to dialogue about them in more detail. By the end, we felt like we were fellow pilgrims on a journey not just into the truth as the object of intellectual understanding, but into a self-transforming Truth that changes our lives. In our small groups, we shared with each other our experiences of, and insights into, what transforms our lives. In this sharing, we celebrated our similarities and accepted our differences as fellow pilgrims. We all felt that humankind around the world needs to listen to the words of their religious traditions and provide a place in their lives for listening to, and responding to, scripture so they can find inner peace and a deeper love for others.

At the end of the dialogue, I was asked again to write the final report. We went to the one computer in the monastery, which was in a small windowless room. Bishop Michael L. Fitzgerald, M.Afr., then Secretary of the PCID, was there helping with the composition, and Ann did the typing. However, the electricity would go out from time to time, and we just sat in the pitch dark room waiting for a monk to fix it. It was actually a nice bonding time with Michael for both Ann and me. We finally finished sometime before morning, and one of the monks took us back to the guest house waving a flashlight on the ground in front of us to scare away any cobras. The next day, the group approved the report with some additions to the text. Ann and I got into a taxi and headed back to Bangalore for a shower, a meal, and a bed.

The Vatican's Third Dialogue with Buddhism: Japan

The Taiwan and India dialogues were in both Buddhist and Catholic monastic settings. So, the PCID decided to hold the third dialogue under Pope John Paul II in a lay setting. They chose the Rissho Kosei-kai as their lay partner in Tokyo for the dialogue in 2002. The participants came from Singapore, Hong Kong, Macao, Japan, India, Myanmar, South Korea, Sri Lanka, Taiwan, Thailand, Italy, and the United States. The theme was "Sangha in Buddhism and Church in Christianity." The agenda included four topics: "Jesus Christ and his Church and the Buddha and his Sangha," "Apostles, Martyrs, Saints, and Doctors in Christianity, and Buddhas, Bodhisattvas, Arhats, and Lamas in Buddhism," "Monastics and Monasteries in Christianity and Buddhism," and "The Laity in the Church and the Laity in the Sangha."

Cardinal Arinze had just been promoted to be Prefect of the Congregation for Divine Worship and Discipline of the Sacraments. So, Michael L. Fitzgerald, who had been elevated to Pro-President of the PCID, gave the opening remarks. Rev. Katsunori Yamanoi did the same as Chairman of the Board of the Rissho-kosei Kai. Then, greetings were given by Archbishop Ambrose De Paoli, Apostolic Nuncio of Japan, Archbishop Peter Okada Takeo, Archbishop of Tokyo, and Cardinal Peter Shirayanagi, Archbishop Emeritus of Tokyo. There were ten Catholic participants and thirteen Buddhists, since they came from so many countries.

The program was structured in ways that were very conducive to dialogue. Each session opened with time for prayerful silence. Each theme was addressed by papers from both a Catholic and a Buddhist, and each speaker had a respondent from the other religion. A lively discussion followed the two presentations and the two responses. Then, the participants were divided into small groups, and each group was given a list of questions about the presentations. This was meant to guide the participants' discussion.

The first theme for discussion was "Jesus and the Church and Buddha and the Sangha." The discussion began with how Catholics view the Church as a people gathered together by Christ as a "sacrament," that is, as a sign and means for the unity of humankind and the unity of humankind with God. The birth and life of the Church is seen as the work of the Holy Spirit wherein Christ is present in the midst of the community and within each person in the Church. Christ gives the members of the Church the grace to live a Christian life though the Holy Spirit. The Church is also described as the Mystical Body of Christ made up of one body with many parts. Christ has given the Church visible sources of grace, called sacraments, that involve God's presence with saving, healing, and forgiving action.

The Sangha was originally formed by the historical Buddha to follow his teachings (Dharma) on the path that leads to Nirvana. The Sangha in this original sense meant the monks and nuns living the monastic life. There is also an expanded meaning of the Sangha that includes laypersons as well as monastics. The monastics guide the laity in understanding and following the Dharma. In turn, the laity follow the Dharma by supporting the monastics. This original form of Buddhism is practiced in South and Southeast Asia. Eventually, another form of Buddhism developed called Mahayana, the "Great Vehicle," that brings people to Buddhahood. Sangha practices developed to help both monastics and laypersons to eventually attain Buddhahood. With this attainment, the Buddhas reside in celestial realms from where they can aid persons in the world, and also host Celestial Bodhisattvas in the later part of their journey to Buddhahood. Mahayana Buddhism is practiced in Central and East Asia. Both forms of Buddhism have also spread all around the world.

The second theme for discussion was "Apostles, Martyrs, Saints, and Doctors in Christianity, and Buddhas, Bodhisattvas, Arhats, and Lamas in Buddhism." The discussion began by presenting how Jesus entrusted his Church to his apostles, sending them into the world to announce the Gospel and establish churches. The successors of the apostles were the bishops of the different churches. The bishops sent priests to nearby churches as the number of Christians grew. The saints are holy persons who are known for their heroic sanctity and are in heaven. While Catholics adore and worship God, they also venerate the saints and ask them to intercede for them before God. A special place among the saints is given to Mary, the mother of Jesus who is known as the "Mother of God" since her son was the incarnation of God. Finally, the doctors of the Church are saints who received a grace in this life to reach a deep understanding that they expounded in their writings, which became foundational for the teachings of the Church.

Buddhism in South and Southeast Asia, known as Theravada (the Way of the Elders), has as its goal the attainment of Nirvana. A person who has reached Nirvana is called an Arhat. They have reached this state by following the Path of Purification that includes morality, meditation, and wisdom as taught by the Buddha. At death, they pass on to Final Nirvana. The Buddhists who follow Mahayana Buddhism, primarily in Central and East Asia, seek to be reborn in this world after death. Their ideal is that of the Bodhisattva who take a vow to remain in this world following a ten-stage path leading to birth as a Buddha in a celestial realm where they continue to help persons in this world. A "Lama" is a term used in Tibetan Buddhism to refer to a monastic who follows the early moral precepts of Theravada, the teachings of the Mahayana Bodhisattva tradition, and the practice of "deity yoga." The latter connects the practitioner with the celestial Buddhas and Bodhisattvas in order to more quickly discover the "mind of clear light" and attain Buddhahood.

The papers on these topics led to lively discussions in our small groups. The Buddhists were especially interested in the Catholic views concerning the communion of saints in heaven and their ability to assist persons in this world. They saw this as similar to the celestial Buddhas and Bodhisattvas bestowing this worldly blessing. In this discussion, the role of Mary in assisting Christians was of special interest to Buddhists from Central and East Asia. They compared her to Avalokiteshvara, a female Bodhisattva known as Guanyin (China), Gwan-eum (Korea), or Kannon (Japan) who plays a similar feminine role in Buddhism.

The third topic was "Monastics and Monasteries in Christianity and Buddhism." Monastic and religious orders have played crucial roles in the Church. Their history began with the hermits in the second and third centuries. Then came the monasteries of the fourth century. In the thirteenth century came a great renewal of religious life: the mendicant orders of the Franciscans and the Dominicans whose members did not live in monasteries, but in small communities among the lay people dedicated to prayer and service to society. This focus on service grew in the sixteenth century with the Jesuits and all the service religious orders of priests and nuns working for the good of society, especially the poor. These new communities provided the faithful places of inspiration and retreats for a deeper spiritual life. The Buddhists were very interested in these communal innovations since they too have had many similar changes in monastic life over the centuries.

Buddhist monastics live in monasteries but have always played a significant role in the surrounding society. Even the early monasteries often had gardens and even playgrounds for children. The monastics provide moral and spiritual guidance and visit the homes of laypersons to provide rituals for their families. In their monastic lives, they give witness to peace, harmony, compassion, loving-kindness, and care for all living beings. Due to this connection to the laity, the monasteries contributed to the creation of Buddhist cultures and arts. Some Buddhist monastics seek a more isolated life for meditation. They often live in nature, especially caves as forest monks.

Finally, we dialogued about "The Laity in the Church and the Laity in the Sangha." All members of the Church are consecrated to God and filled with the presence of Christ and the Holy Spirit through their baptism, confirmation, and reception of the Eucharist. They are "called" in the Church to active participation in the mission of Christ and to growing in their faith through service and prayer in marriage or the single life. Some laypersons join what are called "third orders" connected to the traditional celibate religious orders of the Church. From celibate members of the religious orders, they receive spiritual guidance and participate in spiritual practices and social action. All laypersons are called to put their faith and moral ideals into practice in their work and family life, as well as their community life. They are expected to work for justice, peace, and unity in the world for the good of all. After World War II, a number of lay spiritualties emerged in the Church—a phenomenon that the Church has referred to as a new "springtime." They have different "charisms" or gifts from God for the lay members, single or married, in their communities.

Historically, lay Buddhists follow certain moral precepts in their daily lives, go to temples for rituals, seek guidance from the monks or nuns, and gain good karma for their next rebirth. Some laypeople become monks or nuns once their family is grown. What the group found very interesting is that in Buddhism since World War II, there has also been a greater emphasis on social engagement by both monastic and lay Buddhists working together. This has led to new Buddhist lay organizations. Our host, the Rissho Kosei-kai, is a good example of how laypersons in the *Lotus Sutra* tradition of Mahayana Buddhism in Japan developed methods for moral and spiritual guidance. This has also led them to be engaged in local social action and to work for world peace with other religions. They are an example of what is today called Humanistic Buddhism that has developed in many Buddhist countries. Many of the new Humanistic Buddhist groups have developed connections with some of the new lay movements in the Catholic tradition. Given these connections, the small groups had much to discuss and share about these connections.

By the end of the dialogue, I was again very thankful for the small group gatherings. We better understood and appreciated how the words of Jesus Christ and Gautama Buddha penetrate the actual lives of the participants. We could share concrete examples of how our religious communities provide support, guidance, solidarity, inspiration, and ideals that have certain similarities. We came to feel a kind of kinship with each other as fellow pilgrims with values that are often very similar in daily life. I would say that such dialogue with people from so many countries and cultures gives one a global sense of belonging to one human family. We began to feel like brothers and sisters. It was said by Buddhists and Christians that this is needed in today's world where there is so much division, prejudice, nationalism, racism, and ethnic sectarianism that cause human suffering and do so much damage to our common environment.

Building Bridges of the Heart

I conclude this chapter with a personal experience of bridge-building of the heart that happened after this third dialogue of the Vatican. Before the Tokyo dialogue, Gene Reeves had invited me to his home for a gathering of Rissho Kosei-kai persons involved in English-language translation work. Gene was dean of the Meadville Lombard Seminary at the University of Chicago. He became involved in the Buddhist-Christian dialogue about the same time as I did and later became a member of the Rissho Kosei-kai as a scholar and a practitioner. So, after the dialogue, I stayed in Tokyo to take Gene up on his invitation.

Gene and his wife, Yayoi, lived on a typical narrow street with old-style Japanese houses. He introduced me to Yayoi and to other members of the Rissho Kosei-kai who joined us. At one point, a man shared that he was very upset with the economic situation in Japan that had hurt him financially. The group stopped talking, and individuals began to share their thoughts about his problem based in part on their own experiences and also on the teachings of the *Lotus Sutra*. The *Lotus Sutra* is the central Buddhist text for the Rissho Kosei-kai.

I realized that we had shifted to *Hoza*, or "Dharma Sitting," which is a very strong and unique practice of the Rissho Kosei-kai. I had only read about it. So, I knew that typically persons go to temples and sit in small circles and help each other with their personal problems based on the Dharma teachings of the *Lotus Sutra*. Persons would share their problem, and the leader and others in Hoza would respond to the person in need. In the case at Gene's home, the man who shared about his problem repeated it. The others present then shared their thoughts. The man again repeated himself. This went on for almost an hour. My reaction was, *Why is this man saying his problem over and over?* Eventually, he did stop, and we concluded our socializing.

Later, I asked Gene why this fellow kept repeating himself. Gene explained that *Hoza* is not just a time to share problems, but to be healed of the problem by the Dharma of the *Lotus Sutra*. As long as a person does not feel healed, he or she repeats the problem. He said that if a person is not healed in the Dharma sitting, then someone who is trained will go to the person's home and stay with him or her, continuing the healing process. Gene said that Yayoi does this and sometimes stays with a person who is hurting 24/7 for a week or more. This is really unusual for the Japanese who traditionally do not share their personal issues with others. As a typical American, I asked if the people like Yayoi get paid for their services. He looked surprised and said, "Not in money, but in good karma." As of this writing, Gene has passed away. I lost a brother but still feel him in my heart.

CHAPTER 4

9/11 and Dialogues of the Heart in Central Asia, the Middle East, and North Africa

On September 11, 2001, my daughter Kristen Mitchell was on the F Train going from her home in Brooklyn to her classes at Columbia University in Manhattan. Between the Fourth Avenue and Ninth Street stations in Brooklyn, where the train goes above ground, everyone in the car noticed smoke around the World Trade Center. Kristy thought it must be a small fire. But when she reached the Fourteenth Street station in Manhattan to change trains to Columbia, she realized that all the trains were stopped. She also heard people talking about the World Trade Center but did not understand what they were saying.

Kristy walked upstairs and exited the subway station. She looked south between the tall buildings toward the World Trade Center. The towers were gone! Massive clouds of ash and smoke were coming up the street. She could not believe her eyes and was confused about what happened and what to do. She decided to take a bus going north. The bus was packed with people talking about the situation. They were afraid that what happened was just a first attack, and that there may be more attacks in the city including where they were going. Everyone was really upset and crying. Cell phones did not work, so they felt isolated and afraid.

The bus moved very slowly, so Kristy got off at Twentieth Street and started walking up Seventh Avenue. When she reached Thirty-Fourth Street, she walked over to Oxford University Press, where she had worked before going to Columbia. She wanted to call my wife and me to say she was safe. We talked for a short time, and Kristy went back to Seventh Avenue. By this time, she saw an even larger swirling brown dust cloud, and the people walking north now filled the street, and many were covered in dust and ash. Nobody talked, but just looked stunned. Sometimes people stopped in front of stores that had televisions in the windows to try to understand what was happening

Kristy finally reached her friend Tara's apartment on Ninety-Sixth Street. Kristy and Tara sat in front of the television for the rest of the afternoon. Both were very afraid. They were anxious about what and who might be targeted next. Later, the subways began working again, so Kristy started out taking the trains back to Brooklyn. People on the train were in shock and tears. When Kristy finally got back to her apartment, the windows were open since it was a hot day, and the air in the apartment smelled like something burning, and dust, soot and ashes covered everything. The wind from the World Trade Center area had blown across the East River to Brooklyn, and Kristy's apartment in Park Slope was just up the hill from the water. The soot lingered for days, and the air in Brooklyn was hard to breathe for weeks. The emotional toll was terrible. People were upset and cried with family and friends, especially as the names of those who died were released. Many were police and firemen from Brooklyn.

Soon, stories of heroism began to spread, and people came together to help, console others, and perform heroic acts. Kristy was impressed when she learned that the firefighters in Redhook Brooklyn could not drive into Manhattan. So, they actually ran through the tunnel to get to the site and help. These heroic responses were important to everyone in New York City dealing with the tragedy.

This tragedy that touched persons across America led me to think about what I might do in response. In fact, I had been on the first airplane allowed to fly from Indianapolis to Washington, DC, to attend an interfaith event led by the Catholic Church. Going through airports with guards and police dogs everywhere strengthened my inner sense of being called to do something in response to 9/11. I began to think about how the second Dark Night, that lasted eight years from 1991 to 1999, had come to an end just two years before.[1] During those two years, I felt a new freedom and strength that were not in me before that experience. I also remembered that toward the end of that Dark Night, I felt God calling me to do something for "those most in need with kindness and care."

So, I began to think that perhaps the second Dark Night was meant in part to give me the inner strength and courage to respond in some way to the darkness of 9/11. In fact, as you will read, the dialogue projects we undertook were both strenuous and dangerous. Without the second Dark Night, I would not have been physically, mentally, or spiritually able to engage in these projects.

Early Dialogues with Islam

In 1996, five years before 9/11, John Borelli, who was a friend and fellow scholar of religion at the National Conference of

---

[1] Mitchell, *My Dark Nights*, pp. 58–108 (NY: Herder & Herder/Crossroad Publishing, 2021).

Catholic Bishops, asked me to join in a dialogue they were having with the Islamic Society of North America (ISNA). The national headquarters of ISNA is in Plainfield, Indiana, just an hour or so away from my home. At the first dialogue, I was impressed by the warmth and kindness of the ISNA members, and the positive activities in which they were engaged in the United States. Many of these activities were designed to confront the terrorism of radical Islam, and to keep youth from being influenced by it in the United States.

In 1997, Chiara Lubich was invited by Warth Deen Muhammad, son of Elijah Muhammad who was the founder of the Nation of Islam and its leader from 1935 to 1975, to speak at the Malcolm Shabazz Mosque in Harlem. This was the mosque of Malcolm X, and Chiara was the first Christian and first woman to speak there. W.D. Muhammad and Chiara Lubich had developed a friendship that led to this invitation. She spoke to 3,000 persons in and outside the mosque quoting both the Bible and the Qur'an. After the talk, Lubich and W.D. Muhammad made a "pact" that their movements would work together for unity by building a new brotherhood and sisterhood between their members.

In 1999, the PCID invited W.D. Muhammad and other religious leaders to an interreligious assembly. W.D. Muhammad was the Muslim leader chosen to offer a concluding prayer on the steps of the St. Peter's Basilica. The Focolare arranged this concluding service. Then in 2000, there was a gathering of 7,000 followers of W.D. Muhammad and Chiara Lubich in Washington, DC. Both leaders encouraged their followers to create ways of working together for "Universal Brotherhood/Sisterhood." I have to say that when I entered the hall, the African Americans around me seemed to keep to themselves. But at the end of the gathering, many turned to me and other White persons in the Focolare and started conversations with smiles on their faces. I got to know one man who shared about being in prison and finding Islam. He explained how it changed his life, especially in his family with his wife and children. I shared how I had been a Buddhist and converted to Christianity where I found the Focolare that also changed my family life. We embraced.

I continued to participate in this new dialogue across race and religion in both Indianapolis and Chicago. Eventually, we called our gatherings Encounters in the Spirit of Universal Brotherhood. I attended the weekly lunches with Catholics and African-American Muslims at Shapiros—a Jewish deli. We also had special events in Indianapolis that included persons who had come down from Chicago. At lunch in one of these gatherings, I sat across from an African-American Muslim woman from Chicago. She was a schoolteacher, and we had a nice conversation about being educators and relating to our students. At the end, she said to me, "You are the first White person I have ever talked to."

Being surprised, I asked, "But you must have talked to White people over all these years in Chicago."

She replied, "In stores when I buy things. But, I have never actually sat down and discussed anything with a White person."

Some years later, I spent an afternoon with Imam Pasha at the Malcolm Shabazz Mosque. We met as strangers and left as brothers. Later, we would be on a panel at the Parliament of the World's Religions speaking about the connection between the Focolare members and the followers of W. D. Muhammad. At a meal during the Parliament, someone asked Imam Pasha how he sees Chiara's role in his life as a Muslim. He thought a moment and said, "We are walking the Straight Path of Allah, and sometimes we need some help. I believe Allah drops down ropes for us to use to stay on the Path. I see Chiara as one of those ropes."

In my dialogues at ISNA, I met and came to highly respect its Director, Dr. Sayyid M. Syeed. We became close friends. As president of the Muslim Students Association, founded in 1963, he went on to create ISNA. He also became an advisor for the Council on American-Islamic Relations (CAIR) and is still a leading voice in interreligious dialogue. He was invited to the Vatican by Pope John Paul II, and he led the American Muslim leadership delegation that met with Pope Benedict in Washington, DC. Syeed has spoken about Islam and Muslim issues on NBC, CBS, ABC, PBS, and CNN. He has also spoken on Islam in America on national television networks throughout the Middle East.

His interreligious work includes working with Jewish leaders. He cosponsored the first National Summit of Imams and Rabbis. That same year, he was instrumental in inviting the president of the Union for Reform Judaism (URJ) to address the annual convention of ISNA, and brought a delegation from ISNA to address the annual convention of URJ. Other initiatives included bringing together 100 Muslim organizations and 100 Jewish organizations to hold annual joint events condemning Islamophobia and antisemitism, as well as organizing the first group of Muslim leaders to visit Holocaust sites in Auschwitz and Dachau. Syeed was the person who encouraged me to work with the U.S. Department of State by creating dialogue projects in countries with majority Muslim populations in order to counter radical Islam.

The Indiana Center for Cultural Exchange

In considering Dr. Syeed's suggestion, I remembered the words of His Holiness the Dalai Lama when he told me that the most important thing to do in the future is to work with youth since the violence of the future will come from young persons.

I thought to myself that if we can reach youth through projects that will tie them to their communities, and lead them to respect persons of other ethnic and religious backgrounds, they would be less susceptible to radical recruitment.

So, I called a meeting of faculty members from Purdue University, the University of Notre Dame, Indiana University, and Dr. Syeed from ISNA. At that meeting, we agreed to create the Indiana Center for Cultural Exchange (ICCE), and to seek project funding from the Department of State's Office for Public Diplomacy. Our goal was to work with the Department of State in carrying out peace projects for Muslim youth.

Our partnering organizations grew to include the Prince Alwaleed bin Talal Center for Muslim-Christian Understanding at Georgetown University, the Joan B. Kroc Institute for International Peace Studies at the University of Notre Dame, the World Conference for Religions and Peace, the Parliament of the World's Religions, the U.S. Conference of Catholic Bishops, the National Council of Churches of Christ, the Christian Theological Seminary, the Council for American and Islamic Relations, the Washington, DC, American Muslim Council, the NCAA Hall of Champions, and the American College of Sports Medicine. With this support, our proposed projects were all funded by the U.S. Department of State.

The U.S. Summer Institute for Middle Eastern Youth

When I talked to my point person at the Department of State about our plans to focus on youth, especially through sports, he asked us first to hold a summer institute for youth from the Middle East and North Africa in order to learn more about the lives, values, concerns, hopes, and expectations of Muslim youth. This idea was accepted by the ICCE, so we held the summer institute at Purdue in 2004.

Since the participants were underage, I cannot use their real names. We had a boy from Bahrain, a girl from Egypt, a Muslim boy and girl from Israel, a boy from Jordan, a boy and girl from Lebanon, a boy from Morocco, a girl from Oman, two girls from Saudi Arabia, a girl from Syria, two girls from Tunisia, a boy and girl from the West Bank, and a boy from Yemen. To tell the truth, my wife and I fell in love with all of them! They were wonderful young people, and very smart. Throughout the month of the summer institute, they shared a great deal with us about themselves and their lives in the Middle East and North Africa.

This sharing also took place in the classroom. For example, the students took a course on American political life. The instructor once asked them: "What comes to mind when you hear the word *democracy*?" Their answers included war, killing, people disappearing, lack of food and water, economic distress, etc. They all said that they would like to live in a democracy, but if people try to achieve one too soon it ends in war: "We have to take small steps toward democracy or people break into different factions and we end up in wars."

They loved the class on American music taught by a professor whose expertise at that time was the roots and development of rock and roll, the blues, rap, punk, and post-punk. He taught while walking on the tables used by the students. One student asked me if all professors in America walked on their students' tables. The professor featured music by Elvis Presley, Chuck Berry, Bob Dylan, Jimi Hendrix, Nirvana, and others. The students responded with tapes of the cutting-edge music in their countries, which were quite good. They explained the meaning of the songs given the conditions of their lives and compared their conditions and songs to the conditions and songs of American artists.

Perhaps the most important segment of the institute for the students to bring home with them was Jerry Peters' programs on youth leadership. The programs concentrated on understanding oneself and others to develop healthy relationships across ethnic and religious lines, developing positive and effective means of communication, and understanding group dynamics. Later, we used these techniques in in our projects in Kyrgyzstan, Lebanon, and Algeria.

We took them to an interracial and interreligious soccer match between White Christians and African-American Muslims. Our students joined the games and had long discussions with the African-American Muslims. We also went to Indianapolis to visit the Governor of Indiana, Mitch Daniels, who is part Lebanese. Finally, we took them to ISNA outside Indianapolis for evening prayer at the mosque, a Middle-Eastern dinner, and a presentation by Dr. S. Syeed on Islam in America.

One of the highlights of our visits was at the University of Notre Dame where we had lunch at a Lebanese restaurant and attended a discussion led by Imam Rishied Omar, Coordinator of the Kroc Institute's Program on Religion, Conflict, and Peacebuilding. This discussion on Islam and Islamic culture in the Middle East and North Africa could have gone on forever. Later, we took them to Muhammad Ali's home and training center in Michigan. We spent a good part of the afternoon with Ali. He signed a pair of children's boxing gloves for each student, even though his hand suffered in the process. Each student had his or her picture taken with Ali.

We also took the students to Chicago for an overnight visit to local museums, the Sears Tower, the House of Blues, the Mayor's office, the Focolare Center, and the Mosque Foundation of Chicago. The final visits were in Washington, DC, and from there the students flew home. One day, they visited the capitol building when there were noon prayers for Muslims. Besides sightseeing, they went to Georgetown University for a program that included representatives from CAIR, and the Center for the Study of Islam and Democracy (CSID).

I clearly remember each student. They became a second family for Ann and me. This was a deep experience of the heart. Each one shared their story with us—some were very personal and sad, but all were hopeful about the future. They told us that it was very important to each of them to have us with them as grandparents. Here are some comments by our students about the summer institute:

- **West Bank:** "We learned new things about other people, religions, and cultures in a way that builds unity between us since we are all coping with problems and are following our dreams. We can use all the help we can get to achieve our goals."

- **Tunisia:** "By learning about other cultures and peoples, I learned more about my own culture. We need to celebrate the differences as well as the similarities to leave the world a better place."

- **Egypt:** "I discovered that we are all more similar than different. So, even if we come from different countries and cultures, and have different values and beliefs, we can still become real, lifetime friends."

- **Lebanon:** "Bringing us together given our limited experience and set of beliefs led me to make friends with persons from all over the Arab regions. This kind of brotherhood and sisterhood can be a basis for peace."

- **Bahrain:** "I now know that building positive relations is really important. Our wars of the past were the result of diversity without understanding and respect. We need to help build a more united world where we all speak the language of peace and the value of diversity."

- **Jordan:** "We in the Arab world have some things in common and many differences. The latter can enrich us or divide us. It is not easy to develop a unity of different systems of culture. We need more global minds about the world while enjoying what is precious and positive in each of our cultures. Before we judge another culture or country, we need to understand it, experience it, and live in it. I found that doing this in the USA has changed my view of America."

- **Israel:** "As an Israeli citizen, I have never met persons from the Arab countries surrounding us. But here we all became a family with our differences and similarities. My roommate was from Lebanon, just fifty miles from where I live. We became best friends, and yet I cannot visit him. The world needs to change like we have changed, being together as brothers and sisters with eyes of peace and fellowship."

Building Ethnic Unity and Peace among Youth in Kyrgyzstan

The Osh area in the south of the Kyrgyz Republic extends to both Uzbekistan and Tajikistan. Because of the multi-ethnic population, there have been inter-village conflicts, along with economic decline and unemployment. Therefore, this area had been exploited by the Islamic Movement of Uzbekistan that seeks young recruits to send to Al-Qaeda. Youth, who make up about half the nation's population, are especially vulnerable to ethnic prejudice and violence, making them prime targets for recruitment. We created "Unity Through Sport," or USPORT, to address this risk by promoting constructive youth sports programs with the in-country support of Mercy Corps. Our project to prevent or reduce stereotyping, violence, and hatred among youth took place in the Nookat region of Osh Oblast. Our goal was to help youth feel more connected to their villages, to persons of other ethnicities in their villages, and to the ways of their elders, so that they are less inclined to join terrorist groups.

In 2004, Mercy Corps sent an exploratory group to Osh to secure support from the Islamic University of Kyrgyzstan as well as the Grand Mufti of Kyrgyzstan who is a native of the Nookat region. They also met with the village leaders in the Nookat region who promised hospitality, which also meant safety if Uzbeck rebels were in the vicinity. Mercy Corps evaluated all the sports venues in the villages that were built by the Russians and then abandoned. They began to recruit youth to help repair the basketball and volleyball courts, as well as to build a new soccer field.

We sent Jerry Peters and Imam Rashied Omar to Osh. Rashid met with the area's Madrassas, inviting them to field soccer or basketball teams. Their students are the least educated, since they focus just on Islamic texts, and least connected to the communities—thus the most vulnerable to radical recruitment. Rashied was successful, and they all participated in USPORT. Mercy Corps persuaded women to train to be coaches in order to encourage girls to be on the sports teams. Finally, Mercy Corps invited local boarding schools for orphans to field teams, and we chose a sports teacher from a boarding school for children of parents with tuberculosis to be a USPORT coach.

Jerry Peters and Rashied Omar selected ten USPORT coaches—including Russian, Uzbeck, Tajik, and Kyrgyz men and women teachers and sports trainers—to come to the United States for USPORT training. These individuals were wonderful persons who really cared about the youth in their villages. When they arrived at Purdue, I was impressed by all of them, especially the poorer persons who not only taught school but raised crops at their homes to feed their children. They were amazing human beings and devout Muslims.

The people in that region of Kyrgyzstan are strong persons given the economic situation, rugged physical surroundings, and the need to feed their families in very poor conditions. I felt a great compassion for them and also respect for how they help each other survive and share what little they have. Gulira was the most professional person in the group. She was gracious and committed to giving her life to better the lives of others.

We all felt that under her leadership, USPORT would spread in Kyrgyzstan.

The group that came to the United States to be trained began by spending two weeks at Indiana University where they learned about volleyball, basketball, and soccer coaching. They would train others to be coaches and officials when they returned home. Then, they came to Purdue for what we called "Time Out for Youth" and "Time Out for Unity." We created these short programs to use during breaks at sports practices. Time Out for Youth are programs there were meant to instill life-skills and values to use on and off the court. We also designed them to create community service projects.

Time Out for Unity was more crucial for our projects. It provides times for personal dialogue among the players about their lives. As we would discover, Time Out for Unity provided the very first time the Nookat youth talked about these kinds of personal things with youth from another ethnic culture. The players sit down together and share about themselves, their families, their fears, their personal problems, painful and joyful experiences, and hopes for the future. We found that Time Out for Unity was crucial in building lasting interethnic friendships.

The group went to the Joan B. Kroc Institute for International Peace Studies at the University of Notre Dame. Imam Rashied Omar discussed how Saudi Arabia was building large mosques in Kyrgyzstan and around the world that suppress traditional Islamic cultures and support Saudi theocratic forms of Islam that they call "real" Islam. He discussed how Islam has taken different forms and argued that today, with the diversity of these forms, it is best to have a "co-operative" view respecting the Islamic practices of others. He taught the coaches how to have Time Out for Unity programs where the youth can talk to each other about themselves, their families, and their forms of Islam. The goal is to help them accept each other as Muslim brothers and sisters. He gave the trainers and coaches verses from the *Qu'ran* that stress brotherhood and sisterhood as well as religious tolerance.

The coaches and trainers returned to Kyrgyzstan where Mercy Corps worked with them in nineteen villages to create USPORT-Kyrgyzstan: multi-ethnic sports leagues in three sports with boys' and girls' teams. They also planned "Game Days" that brought together families from the villages to observe sporting events and to watch Time Out for Youth and Time Out for Unity. Thus, the adults were affected by the ideals of USPORT. From their Time Out for Youth, the boys and girls created *subbotniks* (community service projects). The first such project included clearing rubbish, rocks, and weeds from playing fields and building rock barriers around the fields to keep out the wild goats. Our trainers and coaches met with the Imams of Madrasas in all the villages and helped them to field youth teams.

Over one thousand youth participated in the first series of games and projects. The Time Out for Unity dialogues of the heart had a strong effect on the youth. One student said, "These leagues are bringing us from different [ethnic] backgrounds together to discuss our lives and become friends. Now we greet each other in the streets."

Another said, "I am living in a boarding school since my mother and father have tuberculosis. There, we study and work. But now we can play sports and have fun with kids who are different from me!"

One coach said, "After the first soccer game, there was a fist fight between different [ethnic] kids. But after the Time Out for Unity, the kids congratulate each other at the end of the game and even walk together back to the village."

One of the parents said, "At first I was skeptical about this new sports program. But then I saw our son with kids from different ethnic backgrounds becoming friends and bringing them to our house. We met their parents and found that we are more alike than different." Four girls, Russian, Tajik, Kyrgyz, and Uzbek, watched tapes of cheerleaders in the USA and created modest cheerleader uniforms for themselves and danced to different ethnic songs at the basketball games. Also, the *subbotniks* expanded to include volunteers cleaning public areas in their villages, and building rock walls to protect homes and schools from wild animals.

As the months went by, more and more teams were formed in other village schools. This led to tournaments held in the large Nookat City facilities with many people from around the region coming to watch. People from different villages brought food to share with all the kids. Food is not plentiful, so this was really a miracle. Time Out for Unity was affecting the adults in the region. This expansion into other villages, schools, and Madrassas led to a roundtable in Nookat City with school directors and teachers, regional heads of departments of education, coaches, parents, and Imams. All acknowledged the contributions of USPORT including the statistics that showed an increase in school attendance and academic performance in USPORT schools, and a reduction in crime, and ethnic-related violence in USPORT villages.

The outcome of the roundtable was a commitment to sustain the sports programs after the USPORT grant was finished. In fact, we learned that they provided funding for uniforms for disadvantaged families and orphanages. When Imam Bakhadyr of the Nookat Madrassa said that their four soccer teams did not have a training field, the local high schools offered their sports fields. As our USPORT program was completed, we did not worry about the future. The sustainability was strong, and we later found out that the youth participants grew from 1,000 to almost 10,000. Mercy Corps concluded their final report with the following comments:

Given the volatility of the entire Ferghana Valley, the importance of USPORT cannot be overstated, especially considering the particular susceptibility of youth to negative influences such as drugs, crime, and religious extremism. Creating a forum for positive interaction among youth provides the best defense against such influences and is critical in fostering regional stability by linking the youth to their communities, especially those trained in the Madrassas.

Building Intersectarian and Interreligious Unity among Youth in Lebanon

The second USPORT project was in Lebanon from 2005 to 2007, and its goal was two-fold: (1) to improve the technical coaching proficiency, sports management, and the infrastructure of youth basketball in Lebanon; and (2) to enhance coaching methodology to include Time out for Youth and Time out for Unity.

By 2005, a number of destabilizing factors including a multi-religious and sectarian population, a recent history of local and regional violent conflicts, inter-village and cross-border tensions, and economic decline and increased unemployment—had occurred in Lebanon. In this context, Lebanese youth, who constituted approximately 60 percent of the population, were especially vulnerable to the effects of these problems. Unfortunately, basketball, the only thriving sport in Lebanon, had become a focal point in sectarian tension and even violence. Since many basketball games ended in physical altercations, there were more security forces around the courts than fans in the bleachers.

USPORT-Lebanon enlisted the support of the Lebanese Basketball Federation and the Center for Conflict Resolution and Peacebuilding (CCRP) in Beirut. The Basketball Federation sent coaches from different sectors of Lebanon to Indiana for training in USPORT. Later, the Basketball Federation sent the Lebanese Junior National Basketball Team that had just won the Middle East Basketball Tournament. USPORT training in Indiana took place at Indiana University, Purdue University, and the University of Notre Dame following the pattern of Kyrgyzstan.

The coaching delegation went first to Indiana University where their training was led by Joby Wright, assistant coach to Bobby Knight for ten years, a university coach, and a coach of the Harlem Globetrotters. Joby took the coaches to watch games at a junior high school and a high school near Indiana University, and to watch college games at Purdue University and Indiana University. The Indiana Pacers hosted them as special guests at a Pacers game. The Lebanese coaches also visited the NCAA National Headquarters in Indianapolis where they learned about the NCAA's "Stay in Bounds" youth program.

The coaching delegation then went to Purdue for Time Out for Youth and Time Out for Unity training. ISNA hosted the coaches for a program on Muslim-Christian relations, and local Muslim and Christian families hosted them for dinners. In all these situations, we created an environment for a dialogue about the situation in Lebanon. At Notre Dame, the Kroc Institute for International Peace Studies gave presentations on how to assist a country from slipping back into violence after a prolonged period of war. They discussed how countering violence at the grassroots level can be done by sports teams in ways that influence both youth and adults. Rashied Omar, Rabbi Michael

Signer, and Sr. Marianne Farina addressed interreligious ways to reach youth to foster religious tolerance in the face of intolerance from adults.

Personally, I learned many things about the situation in Lebanon. Chafic was from the south and a strong Shi'ite. He had many stories about the Israeli invasions into southern Lebanon. Dany from the Bekkha Valley talked about the situation in his hometown. He said that every family on all sides have experienced the killing of a loved one. Kara and Nazir were close friends even though one was Catholic and the other Sunni. They said that basketball was the link that made their friendship acceptable to others. Roland, a Maronite Christian, was a leader of the Basketball Federation and updated us on the situation in different parts of Lebanon. He said that the Basketball Federation would adjust USPORT to fit each part of the country. All the Lebanese coaches were good people who had their own stories of suffering, as well as their hopes for themselves, their families, and Lebanon.

One person shared that he was driving his car back to Beirut from the south and was stopped by Muslim fighters. When they found that he was a Christian, the leader called a young fighter to take him down the hill and shoot him. As they went down the hill, he talked to the young man about all the suffering and killing he had experienced. The young man stopped, turned around, and went back up the hill. So, he followed. The leader said that the young fighter had lost his brother the previous day. So, if he could not shoot him, then God must want him to live. So, he let him pass and drive to Beirut.

Six months later, after the coaching clinic, we hosted the twelve-member Lebanon Junior National Basketball Team that won the Middle East Championship by defeating Iran, Iraq, Syria, Jordan, and Yemen. Half were Muslim and half were Christian from Mt. Lebanon, Beirut, Tripoli, and Bekkha

Valley. They began with training led by Indiana University basketball coaches. They had a scrimmage session on the Indiana Pacers floor and attended Indiana University and Purdue University men's basketball games. At Purdue, they learned about Time Out for Unity and Time Out for Youth. We took them to Chicago where they were special guests at a Bulls-Spurs game at the United Center. They were jumping with excitement all the way from the bus to the arena.

At the University of Notre Dame, they were asked to break up into small groups of Christians and Muslims and talk to each other about their faith, their family life, and their life with friends. They spontaneously also talked about their hopes and fears for Lebanon. The coaches with them said that players never talk about these things. The players said that they want to lead this kind of Time Out sharing in Lebanon with basketball teams, and also with kids in schools.

When the USPORT coaches and players returned to Lebanon, they trained both coaches and young players. The CCRP translated the Time Out materials into Arabic and produced a workbook in both English and Arabic. They added cartoons to the text, making it more user-friendly. The CCRP passed out the workbook to the new coaches and the youth at USPORT events.

The first USPORT high school event was a one-day players' workshop at Champville High School in Awkar, Lebanon. It was attended by forty youth, ages fourteen through eighteen. USPORT coaches introduced basketball training along with Time Out for Youth and Time Out for Unity. For the latter, the youth gathered in small groups and dialogued about their lives, families, and hopes for the future. In an oral evaluation, all forty students provided positive feedback and requested more dialogue training. Some of the coaches noted that in the sharing about their families, some of the youth began to cry. All the youth had suffered the violence of war and the loss of family members. I would add that at all the USPORT events for youth, many cried. I will always remember a photo I received of a young boy of eleven or twelve sitting on a basketball. He was crying and his coach was kneeling in front of him with his arm outstretched and his hand on the boy's shoulder, talking to him.

The second USPORT event was a coaches' clinic at Balamand University in Beirut for thirty-five young coaches. All the coaches who attended the USPORT programs in Indiana attended this clinic and contributed to its success. They started with the basketball coaching skills they had learned at Indiana University. Then, they presented the Time Out programs, drawing on what they had learned at Purdue as well as from their own experiences when they returned home and coached their teams.

After the coaches' clinic, USPORT held a second players' workshop, this time at Hermel Public High School, in Bekka Valley. There were nineteen players between the ages of sixteen and nineteen. Again, the workshop included basketball training and Time Out training. As with the first players' workshop, the Time Out for Unity had a strong effect on the youth. They expressed a desire to learn more about dialogue and conflict resolution. Even the school officials requested that our coaches repeat this training for other youth in their city who were not basketball players.

USPORT held a third players' workshop, this time at Hripsemiantz School in Fanar, Lebanon. By then, word had spread about USPORT, and seventy-five players between ages sixteen and eighteen came to the event. The program went very well, and for the first time, Hrag Merdinian, a Christian player from Mt. Lebanon, talked about the professional training he had received in the United States. He also spoke about his firsthand experiences of dialogues with other players. Merdinian said that the USPORT experience in Indiana was the first time he had become aware of the way sports can affect one's mind and behavior off the court. He said that he had never really interacted with people from other religious backgrounds prior to his USPORT Time Out for Unity experience. It changed his heart and his relations with other persons.

Soon USPORT-Lebanon reached all five sectors of Lebanon (North, South, Bekkha Valley, Mount Lebanon, and Beirut). It included coaches and youth from all ethnic/religious communities (Shi'ite and Sunni Muslims, Druze, and Maronite, Orthodox, Catholic, and Armenian Christians). All were trained in Time Out for Unity, and the results impressed both the coaches and their communities.

As our two-year grant came to an end, USPORT workshops were taking place in Tripoli and Beirut for both coaches and players. Plus, the USPORT players who came to the United States also presented programs in their own high schools. The program in Bekkha Valley had been so successful that the next one had over one hundred students. Some of the USPORT teams improved so much that they advanced to a higher league. The coaches who came to the United States and those who attended USPORT workshops in Lebanon reported that they were not only more successful as coaches, but also as mentors to their players. The Basketball Federation voted to keep the USPORT program going throughout all of Lebanon.

Sowing Seeds of Peace among Youth in Algeria

For our final USPORT project, we decided to work directly with the government of the country where the project would take place: Algeria. So, our in-country partners were the Ministry of Youth and Sports and the Algerian Basketball Federation. This insured that after our project was complete, it would go forward with strong Algerian government assistance. USPORT Algeria began with an ICCE delegation going to Algeria to introduce the program to coaches and players as well as to the Algerian Basketball Federation. The USPORT head coach was Kent Benson, who was on the Indiana University basketball team that won the NCAA Championship in 1977. He went on to play center for the Detroit Pistons for eleven years. I traveled as leader of the delegation along with three other basketball coaches, one of whom was a woman. Jerry Peters and Nicole LaVoi from the University of Minnesota were with us for the USPORT Time Out training. Jerry worked with the boys, and Nicole worked with the girls. The U.S. Embassy person responsible for us was Amanda Johnson. Upon our arrival, we were greeted by representatives of the Ministry of Youth and Sports as well as the Algerian Basketball Federation, and a number of basketball players. Our arrival was covered by the national media. It seemed USPORT's positive reputation in Lebanon had reached Algeria.

When we arrived, I asked Amanda about a report that Al-Qaida of North Africa had penetrated Algeria. She said that was why we were there—because USPORT was urgently needed. I asked how close they were to us. She said that we did not need to worry since they were in the suburbs of Algiers and we would be downtown. I thought of the Oak Park suburb of Chicago and how easy it would be to get downtown. But, Amanda assured me we would be safe. I saw what she meant the next morning. Leaving the hotel to go to the main basketball arena, we walked between lines of heavily armed soldiers to armored vehicles. I also noticed snipers on the nearby buildings. At that point, I understood why we were instructed not to leave the hotel for any reason!

On the way to the basketball stadium, we also had military vehicles in front and back of us. When the traffic stopped, the soldiers in the vehicles in front of us jumped out and forced the cars out of the way. On another day, our two cars suddenly turned away from the motorcade and went another way to the stadium. I learned that this was in case someone had determined our route and planted a bomb. At the stadium, we were always instructed to run into the building that had snipers on top of it. All this time, as well as in the hotel, I noticed a man with no name tag who was always around watching, but never approached us. Later, I would learn that his code name was "Ferrari." He scared me, but he also made me feel safe.

At our first coaching clinic at the stadium, we were welcomed by the heads of the Ministry of Youth and Sports and the Algerian Basketball Federation. Our arrival at the stadium was covered by the national media. Plus, the Federation gathered all 120 coaches of the basketball teams in northern Algeria. The morning clinic involved basketball fundamentals. A group of Algerian coaches were on the floor practicing the fundamentals that they would teach to their teams. In the afternoon, the coaches watched our trainers do the same training with thirty-three boys chosen from the northern teams. The boys also went through the USPORT Time Out for Unity training with Jerry. The coaches in the bleachers could see that there really was a heartfelt bonding experience.

The next day, the trainers held a more advanced workshop for the coaches in the morning, and in the afternoon, the coaches watched basketball training for thirty-six girls as well as Time Out for Unity taught by Nicole. The girls loved talking to each other about family, friends, school, etc. On the third and final day in Algiers, there was a coaching clinic in the morning to answer questions and address issues that had come up with the coaches and with the boys' and girls' training sessions. In the afternoon, we flew to Hassi Messaoud in the south—in the middle of the Sahara—and were driven to Ouargla with a large military escort. Upon arrival in Ouargla, we had a meeting with the leaders of the Ministry of Youth and Sports, and the Algerian Basketball Federation from the south of Algeria. We stayed in a small hotel in Ouargla surrounded by military troops. Later in the afternoon, we took a well-guarded side trip into the desert to climb the dunes, ride a camel, and enjoy tea in tents. We also visited some shops in the city, and then went back into a desert encampment for dinner with the local leaders. I really loved being out in the Sahara and interacting with the local people. They are good and kind people who work hard for their families in very challenging conditions. And the peace we felt in the desert that stretched to the horizon was tangible and comforting.

For two days, we put on the same coaching clinics in the morning at a small gymnasium as we did in the north. We had fifty-five coaches representing all the basketball teams in the south. The coaches were excellent players . . . especially the women. In the afternoons, we held Time Out workshops for fifty boys and thirty girls. At first, they were shy, but soon opened up and shared from their hearts. We also noticed that a number of youth came into the gym and watched the training both days. The evening of the first day, we were taken into the Sahara to enjoy the sunset and a meal. The next morning, we held another short coaches clinic and a players workshop for the boys and girls who had attended the previous day.

Unfortunately, some new and older youths came into the gym and sat in the stands. Some of them spit on two of our USPORT trainers. The trainers told me, and I told Ferrari who was always with us. He went over to the stands and listened from a distance. Then, he came back to me and said that all of us need to get out of the gym immediately. We picked up our things and ran to the doorway. The older youth from the stands came down and tried to stop us. Ferrari kicked and punched his way through them, leading us to the bus. As we got on board, Ferrari stayed at the door of the bus, kicking those who were trying to stop us. Once we were all onboard, the door closed, and we sped off without the military who were supposed to protect us. Ferrari pointed down a street from where Al-Qaida was expected to arrive and attack the gym. "They missed us by ten minutes," he said. We went to the hotel and then to the airport in Hassi Messaoud to fly back to Algiers.

On the final day of the coaching and players clinics, there was advanced training for the coaches and advanced training and Time Out for Unity programs for boys' and girls' teams. During the Time Out for Unity, Undersecretary of State Karen Hughes arrived with the U.S. Ambassador to Algeria, leaders of the Ministry of Youth and Sports, and the Algerian Basketball Federation. Hughes joined the girls' team in a contest for unity against the boys. When the girls won, they surrounded Hughes and moved in a circle, singing and dancing around her. Hughes loved it and gave certificates to both teams, shaking each player's hand.

That night after dinner, we were all traveling in vans to watch a men's basketball game at a stadium in Algiers. But about twenty minutes before arriving at the stadium, the armored cars and military escort turned around to go back to the hotel. I asked the security official in our car what happened. He said, "We just got word that Al-Qaida has entered the stadium with small bombs."

I asked, "What are small bombs?" He answered that they are bombs just large enough to kill us, but not large enough to blow up the stadium.

On the final evening, we had an official dinner and private meeting with Mustapha Berraf, president of both the Algerian Basketball Federation and the Algerian Olympic Committee. I had negotiated with other officials about the next steps in the USPORT exchanges, but they always told me that in their culture, final decisions were only made by the top person in the company of other leaders. What that top person says in front of the others has to happen or he loses face. So, I met with him in a room filled with the leaders of sports organizations in Algeria and our delegation. We agreed that we would increase the number of coaches sent to the United States from ten to thirty given the success of the USPORT program in Algeria. Mr. Berraf was especially happy with the Time Out for Unity program. He felt that this was needed to keep the youth tied to their communities as Al-Qaida of North Africa was penetrating Algeria.

At this point, I want to say something about my own experience in Algeria. Traveling the country in the north and the south, I met so many good and kind Muslim people who were working hard for a living, and who were raising their families with high moral standards. In the north along the coast and in the Sahara in the south, you find people who are caring for each other according to Muslim customs. For example, I had a conversation with an Algerian coach in Algiers. He said that when the uprisings happened in Algeria from 1988 to 1992, he was asked by his friends to join them in fighting against the government. He was a young basketball coach so was torn between joining the revolt against the government and tending to his basketball team. He decided the latter. The uprising was suppressed, and all his friends who joined the uprising were killed. So, he was thankful for the USPORT training he had received so he could use it with his players to keep them from joining Al-Qaida. Basketball saved his life, and now he could also save others with basketball.

I later learned that members of this rebellion included the Armed Islamic Group of Algeria that beheaded the seven Trappist monks at the Atlas Abbey of Tibhirine. They were like the violent terrorists of the present day. But, I also learned about Emir Abdelkader (1808–1883), who demonstrated a century before what distinguishes a true Islamic military leader following the Qur'an from the terrorist groups of today. He was a very religious Muslim and a military leader against the French invasion of Algeria. His study and practice of Islam guided his actions as a military leader. Abdelkader initiated the first prisoner exchanges with the French and forbade decapitation of French soldiers who were wounded or surrendered on the battlefield. He insisted on respectful treatment of French prisoners, had their wounds treated, and gave them the same rations as his own men. By selecting his caliphs for both their moral and fighting qualities, he enforced other rules of Islamic warfare: no mutilation of the dead, no shooting in the face, no destroying nature, no killing of women, children, old men, or animals (except to eat). Destroying sacred sites and shooting priests and monks were forbidden. He protected Christians and Jews living in Algeria. Once when his army was running out of food, he set the French Christian captives free.

Eventually, the French won and Abdelkader was sent into exile. When he was in Damascus, there was conflict between the Druze and the Maronite Christians. He sheltered a large number of Christians in safe places, including the nuns of the Order of the Mercy Sisters in his own home. His actions during the rebellion and in Damascus gained him acclaim around the world. France and other European and Middle Eastern countries sent him honors. Pope Pius IX awarded him membership in the Pian Order. Abraham Lincoln sent him a gift. Faced with today's terrorist groups, it is important to realize that they are a distortion of Islamic values.

The Algerian Basketball Federation asked the U.S. Department of State to increase the grant to the ICCE so they could send thirty coaches rather than ten to the USPORT training in the United States. The request was granted, and the coaches arrived at Indiana University in time to watch the women's basketball team play the Australian all-star team. They received advanced training for five days with seventeen English-French interpreters. Indiana University gave them a seventy-five-page USPORT playbook in French. At the end of their visit, they watched the Indiana-Alabama men's basketball game.

After the training at Indiana University, we took the Algerian coaches to New Harmony, the historical site of the Robert Owen utopian community in the nineteenth century. Our host was Jane Owen, who provided Halal food and a tour of the spiritual sites in New Harmony. We also had a presentation by a Jew, a Muslim, and a Christian about how they live together in mutual respect and harmony. One coach said, "This is a spiritual place like Fez in Morocco. You can feel a sacred presence that uplifts my spirit and rests my body."

Another said, "The Roofless Church reminds me that we are all children of God under the open sky . . . we are one humanity."

In Indianapolis, we were hosted for dinner by Donnie Walsh, president and CEO of the Indiana Pacers. He talked about how important it is to work with youth in Algeria who might be influenced by radical ideas. We watched the Pacers play the Boston Celtics and were joined by Larry Bird. The next day, we visited the ISNA center and mosque for prayers and dinner and a talk about how radical Islam is not true Islam. The exchange was completed at Purdue with a workshop on leadership of youth, including a manual translated into French, a Purdue men's basketball game, and a farewell dinner.

By the end of the program, I knew all the coaches, and my relationships with them were really heartfelt. We shared about our lives and living our faiths. One coach said, "We all had a distorted view of the United States before we came here. We did not expect people to treat us so well, converse positively about our religion, and go out of their way to help us feel at home. We now feel part of a family."

The United States Embassy in Algiers requested a follow-up exchange that would bring USPORT coaches and trainers back to Algiers to hold a clinic for one hundred coaches and three hundred of their players from all over Algeria. TV coverage was exceptional with reports airing each day and persons being interviewed on a national sports show. Dinners for the delegation were hosted by the Algerian Basketball Federation and by the U.S. Ambassador David D. Pearce at his residence. The ambassador wrote that USPORT was "an excellent example of how the United States can effectively build a more peaceful world though public diplomacy."

Mustapha Berraf sent me a letter thanking me for USPORT: "Not only to reframe basketball in Algeria, but to develop human relations among Algerians and bring peoples together." Ambassador David D. Pearce also sent a letter saying:

> I was extremely impressed with the professionalism and diversity of the delegation under your leadership. I was most impressed with the extraordinary connection established in the course of reciprocal visits between American and Algerian participants. Warm and sincere friendships were made as a result of this program, and they will have a lasting effect. I therefore count your projects as one of the most effective public diplomacy initiatives that I have seen. . . . Your programs of international outreach are an excellent example of how we can build a more peaceful and united world.

After this success, the State Department asked that the ICCE turn our attention to another part of the world where there were active conflict zones: Thailand and the Philippines.

CHAPTER 5

Dialogues for Peace with Muslims, Buddhists, and Christians in Southeast Asia

As our USPORT projects succeeded, the U.S. Department of State began using our program as a model and requested that other universities and sports entities apply for similar sports diplomacy projects. They asked us to expand our work to the southern Philippines and southern Thailand. These regions were conflict zones between Muslims and Christians in the Philippines and Muslims and Buddhists in Thailand. We decided to accept the new challenge and received funding while we were still working in Algeria.

We gathered together the following organizations to join in this new venture: Indiana University, Purdue University, the University of Notre Dame, the University of Chicago, Georgetown University, the Islamic Society of North America (ISNA), the Islamic Center of America, the International Institute for Islamic Thought, the Council for American Islamic Relations, the U.S. Conference of Catholic Bishops, the National Council of Churches, the World Conference of Religions for Peace, the Prince Awaleed Ben Talal Center for Muslim-Christian Understanding, and the All Dulles Area Muslim Society.

In 2008 when the project began, John Borelli, who left the U.S. Bishop's Conference to accept the position of special assistant to the president of Georgetown University responsible for interfaith relations, and I made an evaluation visit to the Philippines and Thailand in January. In the Philippines, we met with U.S. Embassy representatives and our future in-country partners: Macrina Morados, Director of the Institute for Islamic Studies at the University of the Philippines, and Stephen Lo, Director of the School for Oriental Religions who worked closely with Macrina.

We learned about the history of the conflict in the southern Philippines, which was focused in Mindanao. Sunni Islam was brought to the southern islands of the Philippines by Muslim traders in the thirteenth century. Islam expanded north until the Spanish arrived in 1565. They conquered most of the northern Philippines. The Spanish forced Muslims and Jews in the north to convert to Catholicism under the threat of death. They were not as successful in the south where they lost numerous battles against the well-established Muslims. The Spanish referred to the Muslims in the south as "Moros," from the Spanish "Moors." In the early twentieth century, the Americans became involved in conquering the south, leading to the Moro Crater Massacre in 1906.

Eventually, the central government in Manila took control of the south. They then encouraged Christians to move to the south to take over the land. As incentive, the government granted Christian immigrants titles to the land, denying Muslims the land they had occupied for centuries. This takeover was supported by army troops. The Muslim population became landless and poor and were not considered for good jobs by the immigrants.

Then, on March 18, 1968, the Christian Armed Forces killed sixty Moro government army commandos in the Jabidah

Massacre on Corregidor Island. In response, the Moro National Liberation Front (MNLF) was formed the next year with the goal of achieving greater autonomy for the Moros in the southern Philippines through military means. After thirty years of fighting, the MNLF and the government signed a peace agreement in 1998. This agreement created the Autonomous Region of Muslim Mindanao (ARMM) that included two mainland provinces and three island provinces. Meanwhile in 1977, the Moro Islamic Liberation Front (MILF) was founded to achieve greater autonomy for the Moro people. The MNLF agreement left most of the Moro people poor and without good jobs. After fighting for twenty years, a ceasefire between the central government and the MILF was reached in 1997. Negotiations began in 2001, just seven years before our project.

The U.S. Embassy suggested that when we came to the Philippines, our formal delegation should go to the Muslim Salam compound in Quezon City and to universities and Muslim organizations in the Manila area. Then, we should fly down to General Santos City in Mindanao to speak at both Muslim and Catholic universities and organizations. If our effort was to contribute to the peace process, we needed to speak to the leaders and people on both sides. Also, the trip to the south would have a stronger impact on a future peace initiative between the government and the MILF through media coverage. After my experience in Algeria, I asked about protection from the Abu Sayyaf, which was known to kidnap Americans. They said that the government would provide security. So, John and I agreed that we would go first to Manila and then to General Santos City.

After the meetings in Manila, John and I went to Bangkok. We had a meeting at the U.S. Embassy and a day-long meeting arranged by our in-country partner, Prof. Imtiyaz Yusuf from Assumption University in Bangkok, with the following persons:

- Mr. Abdus Sabur, Secretary General, Asian Muslim Action Network based in Bangkok

- Dr. Abdulroning Suetair, professor at Prince of Songkla University, in the southern region of Pattani in the conflict zone

- Dr. Kriya Langputeh, professor at Yala Islamic University, in the southern region of Yala in the conflict zone

- Dr. Niran Pantharkit, professor at Mahidol University, Bangkok

- Dr. Parichat Suwanabhubba, professor at Mahidol University, and a Buddhist leader in Thailand

The professors from the conflict zones in Pattani and Yala gave a history of their regions. For centuries, the area was called the Malay Kingdom of Pattani. Along with what is now Malaysia, it was converted to Islam by Arab traders and became known as an Islamic State in 1457. Then in 1785, the region was defeated by Siam (Thailand). In the 1800s, the region was divided into Pataini, Navathiwat, Yula, Satun, and parts of Songkhia. Given the difficult situation for the Muslims in these regions under Buddhist rule, there arose rebel groups in the 1950s who wanted to separate the Islamic Malay Pattani area from Thailand. But by then, Thailand saw this southern area as a buffer with Muslim Malaysia. The rebel groups were totally separate from each other, so none of them knew what the others were doing. It had been impossible to defeat them. The rebellion had resurgences in 2001 and then in 2004. Thousands died and tens of thousands were injured.

Many Muslims in the south did not support the rebels, and most wanted a peace agreement. Kriya and Abdulroning, representing two of the universities, said the universities wanted peace and to develop peace studies programs to keep young persons from joining the terrorist groups, which now had relations with outside radical groups. John and I agreed that our delegation would go to Bangkok to meet with both Buddhist and Muslim leaders, and then go into the one part of the south where it is safe to visit schools, mosques, and Muslim leaders.

The First Exchange Dialogues in the Philippines

The first exchange to the Philippines was in 2008. Ten of us arrived in Manila and were updated by Macrina and Stephen about the Muslim communities that we would visit in the north and the south. Our group included the following:

- Fr. James Frank Barnett, Dominican specialist on peace and justice issues and our connection to the Dominican University of St. Tomas in the Philippines

- Jamie Bender, specialist at the University of Chicago Center for Middle Eastern Studies and South East Asian Languages

- Zahid Hussain Bukhari, Director, American Muslim Studies Program at The Prince Alwaleed bin

Talal Center for Muslim-Christian Understanding, Georgetown University

- Edward Earle Curtis, Indiana University-Purdue University specialist on Islam in America

- Muneer Fareed, Secretary General of ISNA

- Liese Anne Hilgeman, Program Coordinator for the Middle Eastern and Islamic Studies Program at Indiana University

- Fr. Thomas F. Michel, Woodstock International Fellow, Georgetown University, and former Islam specialist at the Vatican Pontifical Council for Interreligious Dialogue

- Donald William Mitchell, Director of the Indiana Center for Cultural Exchange, and Project Director

- Gerald Ernest Shively, Jr., Purdue Professor of Agricultural specializing in poverty, economic development, and the environment in Southeast Asia

- Rafia Aamir Zakaria, Associate Director of Muslim Alliance of Indiana (MIA), and Director of MIA's Women's Fund

Our first official visit was a meeting with Mayor Sonny Belmonte of Quezon City, where most of the Muslim refugees from Mindanao live. He introduced us to the leaders of the Muslim Consultative Assembly of Quezon City, and a presentation was given by a military general, the top official of the Assembly. He said that the 25,000 Muslims in Quezon City came from Mindanao seeking to live in peace. We then visited the large Salam Compound in Quezon City and were hosted in the compound's public square outside the Madrassa, surrounded by hundreds of men, women, and children. A cultural program was presented for us with songs by children and dances by women. It was joyful and exciting. I was asked to introduce our delegation so they could see we had American Muslims and Christians, and to talk about our mission to support the peace process with the MILF. When I mentioned the latter, the audience stood and cheered.

The next day, we were to visit the Center of Moderate Muslims (CMM) in Taguig City. I should mention that I had developed a personal contact with the MILF. So on our way to Taguig City, our van was contacted and told to park in front of the Gold Mosque, which was nowhere near the CMM. We did so, but there was no one there. We received a second call telling us to go to the Silver Mosque. We did, and we received a third call telling us to follow two motorcycles. Soon, two men on motorcycles drove past us, and we followed them to CMM. We were greeted by beautiful children singing and dancing, and then ushered into the center for a program about their activities given by its president, Professor Taha M. Basman. He was a noted Muslim leader in the Philippines. He talked about their work to counter radical Islamic propaganda, assist the poor in the community, and provide open schools for children. I was very impressed.

Later at lunch, a large man entered the house by the back door. After looking around at everything, he sat next to me at the table. He was one of the leaders of the MILF. People at the table asked him questions about the organization and the peace plan. At one point, I said softly, "I asked you here to see if you can be sure we are safe when we go to General Santos City. We are here in support of the peace plan." He looked at me and then nodded. Suddenly, a man came through the back door, and the MILF leader jumped up and rushed out from the house. We were told to exit the house from the front right away. As we reached the street, we saw troop vehicles a few yards up the street with solders holding machine guns coming our way. The commander saw us and raised his hands to stop the troops. They were after our guest, but he was gone by then. We got into our van and left.

Later that day, we met with President Macapado A. Muslim, who oversees the entire Mindanao State University (MSU) system of eleven campuses. He suggested that one outcome of our exchange could be for the Kroc Institute for International Peace Studies at the University of Notre Dame to help MSU develop peace centers and peace studies programs on each campus. President Muslim described the types of courses they needed to offer and also the kind of outreach programs they needed to provide to the local populations around their universities. He noted that many at and around the universities are Christians who need to be convinced that the peace process is good for them too. He offered to send one of his chancellors on the exchange visit to the United States to pursue this possibility. Given what President Muslim requested of us, I became even more convinced that this exchange could be a lasting contribution to peacebuilding in the Philippines.

The next day, we flew to General Santos City in Mindanao. We were met at the airport by representatives of MSU, General Santos City campus, which was hosting our visit. We went straight to the campus sports arena where we were cheered by an audience of university students in the thousands! All faculty and students were in attendance. We were on a stage at one end of the arena. There were students in the arena seats as well as on folding chairs that filled the floor of the arena. We were overwhelmed and humbled.

The program began with both Muslim and Christian invocations, the singing of the Philippine National Anthem by the MSU Chorale, a welcome address by Abdurrahman T. Canacan, Chancellor of MSU-General Santos, and an amazing choral rendition of "Mindanao" by students who were Christians, Muslims, and members of indigenous religions. We could see that what we had come to present was already happening in Mindanao! The media covered the event for all regions of the Philippines.

We then presented our talks on "Islam in America and Interfaith Relations." This was followed by an open forum where students asked us questions. At the end of the program, we were rushed by hundreds of students with more questions and wanting to talk to us and have their pictures taken with us. We were the first Americans many had ever seen. They were moved by the fact that we had the courage to come to Mindanao and said that our presence meant a great deal to them given the history of that part of the country. One young woman student said in tears:

> Now we know that people know we are here. People are afraid to come down to Mindanao, and I felt like the world had forgotten us. You bring me hope. Thank you for being so brave to come and see that we are ordinary people who want peace and a good life for our children.

Rafia Zakaria, the one young woman Muslim in our group, was swarmed by girls. One said to her: "For us, you are our ideal of a modern Muslim woman. You are a lawyer and a devout Muslim serving your community. We want to be just like you!"

That afternoon, we went to Notre Dame of Dadiangas University (NDDU) for a second program. It was a much smaller university, and the audience of students and faculty numbered around 500. We were welcomed by John Y. Tan, president of NDDU. The program was similar to the one we presented at MSU. But, in addition to the choral programs, there were presentations by Christians, Muslims, and indigenous students. The program concluded with the singing of "The Harmony Song," which was another moving moment in our visit. Again, we talked about Islam in America and its relationship with Christianity through dialogue. For dinner, we were hosted by Datu Tungko Saikol, the Sultan of the Sultanate of Kabuntalan Darussalam, in our hotel for security reasons. The program for the evening included a superb cultural presentation of music, song, and dance. That night, I checked the security at the hotel and found at the back door just one older woman with a handgun sitting and reading a book. I was glad that the MILF was also looking out for us.

The next morning, we traveled to the World Association of Muslim Youth (WAMY) Academy in Bula outside General Santos City. We were given a tour of their Madrassa and a briefing about their educational activities. Besides the Madrassa training, they have women's educational programs, technical education programs, public service projects, and youth peacebuilding projects at the grassroots level. Later,, we returned to Manila and relaxed for the evening. We discussed how impressed we were with the people and institutions—especially the Muslim institutions in Mindanao—and their commitment to dialogue of life experiences between Christians, Muslims, and the indigenous peoples who live in the mountains.

The final day, we went to the U.S. Embassy, where we met with the Philippine government and MNLF officials involved in the peace process. The government representative was Adonis Zeta, Legal Officer for the Office of the Presidential Advisor on the Peace Process. The MNLF leader was Wadi Julkipli. We told them about our exchange visit, and they told us that for the peace talks with the MILF to be successful, there must be more positive involvement in the north of the Philippines where there is more resistance. Any peacebuilding in the Philippines must include educating non-Muslims in the north so they begin to understand and respect Muslims and their culture and history in the South. This is important because the Catholic bishops tell the Catholics in the north not to trust the Muslims.

They said that the press coverage of our exchange program in the north has helped and is bringing liberal religious organizations and universities to work together. They told us that students at the University of Santo Tomas were so energized by what they saw on television, that they joined with the Manila leaders of Religions for Peace to create a new "Interfaith Peace Network" with students from other universities. They came up with the following goals:

- Study sessions for Muslims and Christians to learn more about the history of the Mindanao conflict

- Holding inter-university discussions, press conferences, and activities to publicize the effects of the war situation on families, children and youth, such as poverty, child labor, prostitution, hopelessness, and radicalization

- Building fellowship, solidarity, dialogue, and cooperation among youth of different religions to speak out in support of peace

The Second Exchange Dialogues in the Philippines

The second exchange to the Philippines was in 2009 when we sent only Muslim leaders from America. This was in response to our final meeting during the first exchange when it was emphasized that Philippine Christians in the north need to get to know and respect Muslims. The American delegation of national Muslim leaders could speak to Christian leaders in the north about their positive experiences in the United States with Christians, and they could also speak to Muslim leaders in the north about what might work best for them to influence Christians. Plus, the American Muslim organizations they represented wanted to provide financial assistance to Muslims in the Philippines. So, we sent the following:

- Imam Kareem M. Irfan, of ISNA as the leader. He is also president of the Council of Religious Leaders of Metropolitan Chicago and has been chairman of the Council of Islamic Organizations of Greater Chicago serving over 400,000 Muslim Americans.

- Imam Mikal Ibn Oliver Saahir, of Mosque Cares, the African-American Muslim organization of W.D. Muhammad, the son of Elijah Muhammad, the founder of the Black Muslim Movement. He also serves on the Interfaith Alliance of Indianapolis.

- Imam Abdullah Bey El-Amin, of Mosque Cares and the African-American Muslim community of Detroit, Michigan. He is Imam at the Muslim Center of Detroit.

- Mr. Wael F. Alkhairo, of the All Dulles Area Muslim Society (ADAMS), one of the largest Muslim mosques in the United States serving over 25,000 members in the Washington, DC, area.

- Ms. Rafia Aarhir Zakaria, of the Muslim Alliance of Indiana (MIA). She is the first Pakistani-American woman to serve as a director for Amnesty International USA.

- Ms. Rana A. Irfan, of the Woman's Program of Mosques in Chicago. She is also a member of interfaith initiatives and social outreach programs of the Council of Islamic Organizations of Greater Chicago.

The first event was a roundtable discussion with Muslim leaders from the north. Each leader was selected by their Muslim organizations. Imam Irfan began by sharing a touching message of condolence to the Muslims of Mindanao and in the north on behalf of American Muslims and ISNA. The other delegates shared their rationale for coming to the Philippines at that time when peace negotiations were going on with the MILF. The Muslim leaders from the Philippines shared about issues affecting Muslims in their country, and the American Muslim leaders shared about the issues they face in the United States.

The highlight of the roundtable was the discovery of common ground between Philippine and American Muslims in opposing extremist views, and seeking peace and wellbeing for their communities. It was noted that Muslims in America have a more supportive interfaith environment—something that is still needed in the Philippines. The Philippine Muslim leaders expressed admiration for the American delegation, and they expressed the need for Muslim institutions and organizations in both countries to create links that further anti-extremism education and promote peacebuilding. All agreed to work together to strengthen dialogue among Muslims and non-Muslims in the Philippines in support of the peace process. This meeting led to an agreement between the Philippine leaders and ISNA, with ISNA offering to fund their leaders to engage in outreach programs to Christians in the North.

The second event was a "Public Forum on Islam in America" at the University of the Philippines. The audience was very large and included both Christian and Muslim leaders as well as representatives of the new student organizations that were the result of our first visit. Al-Khairo shared about the experience of how his Mosque and community in the Washington, DC, area relate to Christians as well as to the local and federal governments. El-Amin spoke about the history of the

African-American Muslim experience and of its status today. Finally, Zakaria spoke about Muslim women in the United States and their issues and roles in the American Muslim communities. The public forum was considered by the audience to be a great success.

The third event was a meeting with the National Department of Education officials responsible for the Madrasah Education Program (MEP) in the Philippines. The officials were especially interested in speaking with Rafia Zakaria and Rana Irfan given their experience in Muslim schools in the United States. The director of MEP said that the meeting would be a great help to them as they developed educational policy and materials intended to keep Muslim youth from being influenced by radical Islamic groups. ISNA promised to send educational materials and funding. This was a very promising outcome of the exchange.

The fourth and final event included a visit to the Islamic Studies Call and Guidance (ISCAG). This is a famous school in the north with hundreds of Muslim elementary and high school students from all over the country living in dormitories. It is the most influential Muslim institution in the country. They have also created other schools in recent years. The highlight of ISCAG visit was a public forum on "Islam in America" attended by all the students, faculty members, and parents. Imam Kareem and the other members of the delegation assured ISCAG of their support in terms of linking them to U.S. institutions that could help them improve their Islamic curriculum and provide additional books and instructional materials and improve their classroom and dormitory facilities. ISCAG operates schools that incorporate Islamic Studies as part of their regular government-approved curriculum. They believe that "Teaching Muslims to be Good Muslims" will negate radical ideas and will promote peace.

A Story from the Philippines

Finally, many of the Muslims we met had very touching stories about the conditions in which they live. But one of them stood out and has continued to inspire me for the rest of my life. The story was about a young woman that I will name Isha. I first met her at the University of the Philippines. I was in the doorway to an office of the Islamic Studies Center talking to people inside. Suddenly, they looked to my left and welcomed Isha. I turned and she was right beside me . . . but she had arrived next to me in complete silence. And later, she disappeared in silence. It reminded me of a man I met in Thailand who was once the leader of the armed Communist resistance in the jungles. He moved silently like Isha and saw everything around him, able to judge everything and everyone at a glance.

Isha was the daughter of a leader of the MILF. As a very young girl, she took messages to her father in the jungle. As she grew, she took weapons. At a certain age, she went to join a MILF group at a jungle camp. When she arrived at the camp, the fighters had left to pray, leaving a few older men cooking. Suddenly, a group of Catholics with machetes broke into the camp and started killing the few who were there. One swung his machete at Isha's head and cut off part of her scalp. An older man came into the room and held the man's arms from behind and told her to run. She got away, but at one point turned around and saw the Catholic cut off the old man's head.

For years, she fought with the MILF. They would attack and then disappear by boats, traveling a long distance from the attack site. They would remain hidden for months before returning. She taught herself to read by picking up newspapers and magazines. At one point, she asked her father if she could go to college to be educated. He agreed. But the college she wanted to attend was Catholic and would not accept her since she was a Muslim with no formal education. A call from her father to the president of the college got her admitted. She took classes, and when called by the MILF to fight, she would tell her professors that she would be gone for two weeks. They never said no.

Once, she saw a Bible in the library. When she tried to check it out, they would not let her because she was a Muslim. So, she stole it. As she read the New Testament, she began to cry. She realized that the teachings of Jesus were wonderful and aligned with her understanding of the right way to live as a Muslim. She concluded that the brutality she received and saw from Catholics was opposed to the teachings of Jesus.

When Isha finished her studies at the college that was more like a high school, she joined a Protestant group that built houses for the indigenous tribes that lived in the mountains. Macrina convinced her to come to the University of the Philippines to complete her formal education. That is where I first saw her in the doorway. After completing her studies, she returned to the task of providing housing and other needs to the indigenous tribes. She told me that at first, the tribal people did not want to sleep inside the houses since they had always slept under the trees looking up at the night sky. Eventually, they took palm branches into their houses and put them on the ceiling. With the windows wide open, that worked. She invited me to go into a mountain jungle to visit a tribe. They would take me up on a motor scooter for miles. Also, while I was at the tribal village, an elderly woman would sing day and night for me until I left. She promised that I would eat well and be happy. As I get older, I think I should have taken the invitation.

When Isha was in meetings with us in the United States, I noticed that she knew everything going on around her. If I was at a conference table and something happened, like a member of our delegation falling asleep, I would just look at her. She would look at me, then look around, get up, and take care of what needed to be done without my saying a word. Isha was a wonderful young Muslim woman dedicated to peacebuilding in the context of doing good for the poor indigenous people in her country by providing shelter and food.

Besides Isha, many of the others we met were dedicating their lives as Muslims to helping those in need and contributing to the peace movement, and each had a moving story to tell. In this regard, I would mention that Macrina was approached by two U.S. Army officials outside the Washington, DC, airport before flying back to the Philippines. She had been part of our exchange group. She was given a plaque honoring her for helping the U.S. Army save people in the Philippines after a typhoon. She had been a translator for them for weeks and would also locate persons who needed help. How they knew that she was at the airport in Washington, DC, on that day, I have no idea.

The Exchange Dialogue in Thailand

There was only one exchange visit to Thailand. Our first visit to the Philippines in 2008 was to be followed by our first visit to Thailand. But Thailand was in political turmoil, and the airports were closed due to demonstrations. So, we had to cancel that trip. The members of the second exchange dialogue to the Philippines were able to go on to Thailand. The delegation included the eight U.S. Muslims who attended the second Philippine exchange and three members who joined them for the second leg of the journey:

- Dr. Zahid Hussain Bukhari, director of the American Muslim Studies Program at the Prince Alwaleed bin

Talal Center for Muslim-Christian Understanding at Georgetown University

- Fr. Leo D. Lefebure, the Matteo Ricci Professor of Theology at Georgetown University and a specialist on religion and violence

- Professor Hal Robert Culbertson, Executive Director of the Kroc Institute for International Peace Studies at the University of Notre Dame

The first meeting of the full group was at Horoon Mosque in Bangkok for evening prayer, followed by dinner at a nearby restaurant. While at the mosque, our group learned of the history of Islam in Thailand, the status of the Muslim community in Thailand, and the situation in the conflict region in the south of Thailand. The next meeting was a public forum on "Islam in America" at the Islamic Center of Thailand. It was attended by hundreds of Muslim leaders in the Bangkok area. Imam Kareem Irfan opened the discussion with an overview of the history and recent growth and development of Muslims and active Islamic organizations in the United States. There was a great deal of interest in the status of U.S. Muslims, and the fact that the speakers were American Muslims gave credibility to the presentations. They also wanted to know how American Muslims deal with the radicalization of their youth. Mrs. Huwaidiyah Pitsuwan Useng, secretary to the Minister of Social Development and Human Security in Thailand, encouraged the American Muslims to help them with anti-radicalization and peacebuilding in the south.

The final meeting was with the government's Office of Islamic Affairs. Again, delegation members shared about their experience as Muslims in the United States. The Thai government officials were especially interested in the Muslim-Catholic dialogues in the United States both before and after the events of 9/11. Their office was trying to address the problems in the south by dialogue and were seeking suggestions for success. This discussion was very helpful to the government officials.

Finally, the delegation was able to fly to Nakhon Si Thammarat in the south. They were greeted by Governor Teera Mintrasak, Thailand's first Muslim governor. The delegation visited the Islamic Santhitham Foundation School, spoke with the administrators and teachers, and gave talks to the hundreds of students at the famous school. All the teachers and students were especially interested to learn about Islam in the United States. That evening, the delegation went for prayer at the Sawlahuddin Mosque followed by dinner, and a visit to the Night Market, with stalls owned by Muslims.

The delegation spent the night in Nakhon Si Thammarat and the next day visited the famous Prateepsasana Islamic School, a highly respected private school for Islamic education. It was founded in 1941 as a co-ed school and today has 73 teachers and more than 1,400 students. Its courses go through high school. They also have a business administration school. The Muslim community in southern Thailand is struggling to catch up with social changes, economic development, and modernity. The mission of the school is to offer a modern education that also tends to the students' moral and ethical wellbeing and gives them confidence in their Islamic heritage. The school held an assembly for our delegation, and more than 1,000 students attended, along with teachers and administrators. A group of girls sang for the delegation, and then a chorus of boys sang and performed a dance with music. The delegation presented a short talk about Islam in America, and the children asked many questions. The delegates representing national organizations in the United States reached an agreement with the school to provide books and other education materials to assist in their mission. After visiting the school, they flew to Bangkok.

On the last day, an event was held at Mahidol University in Bangkok for faculty and students. There was a discussion about interreligious dialogue with members of the delegation and the university. Zahid Bukhari presented an overview of Islam in the United States and its engagement in interfaith dialogue with Jews and Christians. Wael Al-Khairo discussed the ADAMS Center, its experience of dialogue in Washington, DC, and its cooperating with the government to combat radicalization in Muslim communities. Rana Irfan made a presentation about Muslim women in Chicago and their experience of dialogue with other religions including Buddhism. Leo Lefebure discussed the Society for Buddhist-Christian Studies as an example of a successful academic dialogue. A lively discussion followed. The students spontaneously applauded, and the question-and-answer period was very long and animated. I would say that as in the Philippines, the Thai youth are very much interested in interreligious relations to build unity and peace in their country.

The final days in Thailand were devoted to discussing what would be a "Regional Peace Education Development Workshop," based on the needs expressed in the Philippines. Before the delegation arrived in Bangkok, Hal Culbertson had met with President Muslim of the Mindanao State University system as well as presidents of three Catholic universities in Mindanao. It was helpful to the Catholic universities in Mindanao that Hal was from the University of Notre Dame. They discussed the need for regional peace education workshops. The Catholic universities in Mindanao said that once trained, they would also work with Catholic universities in the north of the Philippines.

Dr. Mark Tamthai of Payap University in Chang Mai agreed to host the workshop, and Hal agreed that the Kroc Institute would teach the workshop. They all decided that the workshop would teach how to create peace studies courses at their universities that will be required by all students and how to create outreach programs for peacebuilding in the broader communities. The latter was important because while students are interested in peace studies, interreligious dialogue, etc., the middle-aged and older generations are suspicious. Leaders from the Thai universities in the south agreed to participate in the workshop.

Exchange Dialogues in the United States

Besides the exchanges in the Philippines and Thailand, we hosted two return exchanges to the United States in 2008 and 2009. Each had representatives from the Philippines and Thailand. For both visits, the first event was on countering radical Islam and took place at the National Headquarters of the ISNA. ISNA's advice for countering radicalism included the following:

- Reaching out to youth, emphasizing the importance of freedom, education, and economic development

- Training youth in leadership and mentoring them in moderate Islam

- Holding youth conventions and summer camps supporting "True Islam"

- Holding conferences for adults to give them guidance for mentoring their children

ISNA's advice for countering radical writings and ideas included the following:

- Contextualizing passages from the Qur'an that are quoted by radicals

- Discussing the environment in which radicals wrote their views, and explaining why they took radical paths

- Relating radical ideas to circumstances (social and economic) to show that the ideas are not Islamic, nor worth dying for

- Stressing that the Qur'an and its accepted interpretations are more important than texts by radical writers

ISNA agreed to send information to the guests on how to give this advice in the Philippines and Thailand, translate what they send, and make it accessible online.

We then went to the Kroc Institute for International Peace Studies at the University of Notre Dame. Imam Rashid Omar made the following important points concerning how to carry on a discourse with Muslims who are supporting, or are thinking of supporting, radicalism:

- Stress Qur'an 5.9: "O ye who believe! Stand out firmly for God, as Witnesses to fair dealing, and let not the hatred of others to you make you swerve to do wrong and depart from justice. Be just: that is next to piety; and fear God, for God is well-acquainted with all that ye do."

- Stress that deeds are more important than beliefs in the Qur'an. So, test one's beliefs by seeing where they go in terms of deeds. Ask the question: "Do radical views lead to righteous or unrighteous deeds?"

- Stress that mercy is more important than justice; it is the main trait of God, the All Merciful. Radical Islam focuses on justice, and mercy is pushed aside. Justice is reduced to revenge. We need justice that is merciful, not violent revenge.

- Muslims involved in terrorism do so because of political and social problems, not because of religion. Suicide bombers are not acting out of religious fervor, but in reaction to what had happened to them, their families, communities, or nations. Islam is then used to justify forbidden actions for revenge. But true Islam is peace, and a true Islamic reaction involves a non-violent call for justice and mercy from all sides.

- Emphasize that in the Mecca verses of the Qur'an, God does not allow violence. In the Medina verses he does, but only for defense, and one must "protect churches, synagogues, and monasteries."

On our visit to Chicago, we took our groups to The Mosque Foundation on the south side of Chicago with a membership of 50,000 persons, and with prayer services attended by 5,000 persons. We were hosted by Imam Jamal Said, Imam Sh. Kifah Mustafa, and President M. Zaher Sahloul for prayers, a luncheon, a discussion, and a tour of one of their schools. Our participants could see for themselves the new kind of mosque in the United States, one with a community center, youth programs, weekend schools, a girls' school, a mixed school, a food pantry, and counseling services for youth, adults, and women. The community is involved in interfaith dialogue with Christians and Jews in Chicago. There is a women's interfaith group of Catholics, Muslims, and Jews that has been meeting for years and is very successful at building unity.

At the KAM Isaiah Israel Congregation, Rabbi David Sandmel, Crown Ryan Professor of Jewish Studies, spoke about his participation in an international organization called "Rabbis and Imams for Peace." Members of his congregation presented "The Chicago Coalition for Inter-Religious Learning" (CCIRL), a group of Catholics, Jews, and Muslims who work together to evaluate the treatment of the three religions in textbooks, curricula, and teacher training in Chicago.

Our next visit was to Dearborn, Michigan, which has a very large Muslim population. We took our guests to The Islamic Center of America. After a tour of the Shi'ite mosque, Imam Hassan Qazwini met with the participants in his office to answer questions. Afterward, we took a guided tour of the Arab American National Museum that records the history of the experience of Arab Americans in the United States to the present day. The group then enjoyed a museum-hosted luncheon for the group and a viewing of the movie *Journey to Mecca in the Footsteps of Ibn Battuta* together with an audience of Muslim Americans.

We then traveled to Washington, DC, to be hosted by Georgetown University. John Borelli coordinated the schedule for the week. The Alwaleed bin Talal Center for Muslim-Christian Understanding (ACMCU) at Georgetown hosted two panels on Islam in America. Dr. Zahid Bukhari, who directs the American Muslim Studies Program at the center, presented the results of his surveys of American Muslims, which demonstrated that American Muslims are settling into American life like most other immigrant groups while retaining their religious and cultural heritages and shaping these to be consistent with the perspectives of a pluralistic society. This was important for the participants to hear since the American Press often seems to present negative views of Muslim communities, tying them to radical Islam, which is false.

Members of the International Institute of Islamic Thought (IIIT) were present and were impressed with our participants, so they invited them to their institute for an afternoon. Dr. Abu-Bakr hosted the group and introduced them to the work of IIIT. Various institutions are located at IIIT, including The Fiqh Council, which explores relations between Shariah and American life. The emphasis at IIIT is the incorporation of various social sciences into Islamic thought. The IIIT promised to send materials, journals, and books to each of our participants' organizations.

We went to ISNA's Office for Interfaith and Community Alliances, hosted by Sayyid M. Syeed, who at the time engaged in advocacy and lobbying for Muslim interests in the United States Congress. Syeed generated a discussion about what each of the participants were doing in their countries. He then collected the contact information from each person doing projects in Thailand and the Philippines, promising them ISNA's financial help for their social service projects.

One full day was devoted to a program with officers from the World Conference of Religions for Peace (WCRP), which includes Religions for Peace (RFP), that is active in the Philippines. Kyoichi Sugino took responsibility for planning and shaping the day. Joining him were Leonid Kishkovsky of the Orthodox Church in America; Judith Hertz, co-chairperson for Interreligious Affairs; Union for Reform Judaism; and Kinza Ghazanivi, who coordinates youth and women's activities with the WCRP. All of their sessions were very helpful to our participants.

Why am I giving all this inside information about what took place in the United States? First, I want to convey the truth about Muslims in America and in Asia. We found them to be brothers and sisters who spoke from their hearts about their lives, their sufferings, their families, and their hopes for a better world for us all. They also have to deal with the rise of a small minority of their fellow Muslims who have twisted their faith into something evil. I shared with them that this twisting of faith is what we experienced as a violent distortion of Christianity in America with the rise of the Ku Klux Klan. Each clan member was required to join and attend an Evangelical Church to be a good Christian, but what they did to those who were different from them was just as horrible as what radical Muslims are doing today. Second, it is a way of sharing how interreligious dialogue based on the heart, seeking peace between people of different faiths, can be successful.

Also, I wanted to inform readers that for decades, Jewish, Protestant, Catholic, and Muslim leaders in the United States have been working together for mutual understanding and appreciation. This effort has led us to a sense of brotherhood and sisterhood that I will discuss in the next chapter. Stories about these efforts are often ignored by the press in the United

States, which creates misunderstanding in the United States and around the world. This misunderstanding was dismissed by one of our guests, who said:

> We now believe that America can be a new light for true Islam, which means Islam based on the Qur'an and Sunnah can flourish in the freedom of America, rejecting the cultural and patriarchal beliefs and customs of other Muslim countries. . . . Muslims in the U.S. will be likened to the "Madinah" during the time of the Prophet Mohammed, peace be upon him. You have White Americans, African Americans, Asians, Middle Eastern, Africans, Europeans, and many more present at Islamic prayers. Women were also visible during daily prayers. I was really touched by this phenomenon. . . . Exposure to Jewish and Christian communities gave me a better understanding of their positive relation to Islam in a way that can be a model for the world.

And I would add that the heartfelt environment in which all these encounters took place was one of care and respect for one another and compassion for those who suffer discrimination in America as well as in Thailand and the Philippines. Finally, and perhaps most importantly for the future, the exchange visit to the United States led to these specific initiatives for the Philippines and Thailand:

- ISNA agreed to provide the Philippine government's Madrasah Education Program educational materials to support peacebuilding for the curricula for all Madrasahs in the Philippines.

- ISNA agreed to provide books and instructional materials to ISCAG in the Philippines to guide Muslim youth away from extremist views.

- ISNA agreed to provide the Prateepsasana Islamic School in Southern Thailand with books and other educational materials on positive Islamic values, culture, and identity.

- The International Institute for Islamic Thought in Washington, DC, agreed to provide Islamic universities in Thailand and the Philippines with books and journals on Islamic values and cultures from a positive and moderate point of view.

- Members from the Philippine Embassy in Washington, DC, met with our Philippine participants after their Public Forum. They suggested the participants present an expanded version of their Public Forum at different universities around the Philippines, from Luzon to

Mindanao. Martha Buckley, Cultural Affairs Officer at the U.S. Embassy in Manila, suggested they apply for a grant to fund such a lecture tour.

- After seeing the Muslim Cultural Center in Dearborn, the Muslim participants from the Philippines said that they will collaborate with the government to establish two Moro Cultural Centers, one in the north and one in the south, that present the history and culture of the Bangsamoro people. It would educate both Muslims and non-Muslims, especially children, to understand and respect the Moro culture and religious values. American funding will come from ISNA.

- The main initiative was, of course the agreement by The Kroc Institute to present a Regional Peace Education Development Workshop at Payap University in Chiang Mai.

The Regional Peace Education Development Workshop

The final project of the ICCE with the U.S. Department of State was the Kroc Institute's Regional Peace Education Development Workshop at Payap University in Chiang Mai from October 17 to 22, 2010. Following the discussions during the exchange visits, the focus in the workshop sought to enable academic institutions in areas of conflict in Thailand and the Philippines to develop programs that promote peace through their curricula, while also pursuing peacebuilding efforts in their broader communities. The number of participants that attended the workshop included the following:

- Sixteen participants from the Mindanao State University system

- Three participants from the three Catholic universities in Mindanao that are members of the Catholic Peacebuilding Network

- Two participants from the Institute for Islamic Studies at the University of the Philippines

- Ten participants from Southern Thailand (Yala Islamic University, and Prince of Songkla Universities in Pattani and Hat Yai)

- Three participants from Nepal's Tribhuvan University, who asked to participate due to problems from terrorists on their open border with India

- Five workshop leaders from the Kroc Institute at the University of Notre Dame

- Two specialists in peacebuilding in Thailand from Payap University

After the workshop, the participants returned to their universities and created peace studies courses. The universities began teaching these courses in 2011. They began presenting the outreach programs to the broader communities by January 2012. MSU students at all their campuses are required to take a peace studies course for graduation. This is the same at Yala Islamic University, which adopted a peace studies requirement for all students. Prince of Songkla University's two campuses in the south of Thailand offer peace studies courses as electives. Tribhuvan University in Nepal improved its curriculum for its peace studies program. Through the broader community outreach programs at the universities in Mindanao, southern Thailand, and Nepal, the local communities, mosques, temples, and churches developed their own peacebuilding programs.

MSU has 70,000 students enrolled at their campuses in Mindanao. Prince of Songkla University in Hat Yai has 17,000 students, and in Pattani has 10,000 students. Tribhuvan University, one of the largest university systems in the world, has over 200,000 students at campuses across Nepal, and Yala Islamic University, the only Islamic University in Thailand, has 2,000 students. Therefore, every four years, up to one million students benefit from the results of the Kroc workshop. The outreach programs also reach thousands of people in the communities served by the universities.

Finally, Professor Macrina Morados wrote me a letter from her Institute for Islamic Studies, saying:

> Your Chang Mai workshop contributed to actions in the Philippines that played a vital role in the educating

and inspiring the Philippine government and the MILF in their work for a lasting peace agreement. It also educated and inspired the Philippine people to support their work. The lasting fruit is that in less than four years after the workshop and the creation of peace centers around the country, the Philippine government and the MILF signed a peace agreement on March 27, 2014, that granted greater autonomy than the MNLF peace agreement. The MNLF agreement was replaced with the MILF agreement that has provided a much larger, more prosperous, and better funded autonomous region called Bangsamoro.

CHAPTER 6

Pope Francis's Interreligious Dialogue of Fraternity

Pope Paul VI founded the Secretariat for Interreligious Dialogue (SID) on May 17, 1964, to advance the Church's relationship with other religions. In 1988, Pope John Paul II renamed it the Pontifical Council for Interreligious Dialogue (PCID). In 1984, SID identified four types of interreligious dialogue:

- The *dialogue of life*, where people strive to live in an open and neighborly spirit, sharing their joys and sorrows, their human problems and preoccupations

- The *dialogue of theological exchange* where specialists seek to deepen their understanding of their respective religious heritages, and to appreciate each other's spiritual values

- The *dialogue of religious experience,* where persons, rooted in their own religious traditions, share their spiritual riches with regard to prayer and contemplation, faith, and ways of searching for God or the Absolute

- The *dialogue of action*, in which Christians and others collaborate for the integral development and liberation of people

It is important to note that these four kinds of dialogue are not entirely separate. Contacts in daily life will sometimes open the door to the dialogue of action for cooperation in promoting human and spiritual values, as well as the dialogues of theological exchange and religious experience.

After Pope Paul VI's founding of an office for interreligious dialogue, it was the monastics who first took the dialogue forward with Buddhism. In 1974, Cardinal Sergio Pignedoli, president of the Secretariat, wrote to Benedictine Abbot Primate Rembert Weakland urging Christian monks and nuns to pursue mutual understanding with Buddhism. Benedictines had been pursuing East-West Intermonastic Conferences since the one in Bangkok in 1968 where Thomas Merton died. This began a long series of intermonastic Buddhist-Catholic dialogues and exchanges by Monastic Interreligious Dialogue (MID) in the United States, and Dialogue Interreligieux Monastique (DIM) in Europe.

Pope John Paul II became pope in 1978 at a time when the Catholic Church's interreligious dialogue was beginning to develop around the world. His view of the goal of such dialogues was the development of mutual understanding and appreciation. The move to add the focus on theological dialogue to the dialogue of religious experience was a natural evolution involving non-monastics around the world.

The year 1995 was also an important turning point in the Church's theological dialogue for "mutual understanding and appreciation" with Buddhism. For the first time in history, there was a direct dialogue between the Vatican's PCID and Buddhist leaders from around the world. I have described this dialogue in Chapter 3 and elsewhere in this book. Through these dialogues, the Church found a deep "enrichment," to use John Paul II's word. We celebrated our similarities and accepted our differences with respect. These dialogues also gave the Church a better understanding and appreciation of the distinctive messages of Jesus Christ and Gautama Buddha.

The dialogue of mutual knowledge and enrichment has been practiced for decades. It has facilitated the Catholic Church's growth in understanding and respect for the beliefs and practices of the major religions of the world. Under John Paul II, this dialogue also led to closer collaboration between the Catholic Church and other religions for world peace. Pope John Paul II also added the World Days of Prayer in Assisi that took place in 1986, 1993, and 2002. The 1002 Days of Prayer followed 9/11.

Cardinal Ratzinger strongly believed that serious interreligious dialogue derives from a "longing for truth." He believed that this longing is found in every religion. It is what Catholics have in common with persons of other religious traditions. Indeed, *Nostra Aetate 2* teaches that there are elements of the truth in all cultures and faiths that Catholics have a responsibility to "recognize, preserve, and promote." This "deep dialogue" is more than a dialogue conference or an interreligious discussion. For Cardinal Ratzinger, it was exploring together in dialogue *over time* as fellow pilgrims in an *ongoing* journey to a fuller understanding of the truth. In fact, he writes that in so doing, the tradition of the other and our own tradition will be "purified by the truth." It was his belief that such deep dialogue would show us unity in the midst of our divisions and contradictions.

As Pope Benedict XVI, he went on to assert that in this journey, fellow pilgrims listening to the Logos and being purified by the truth also advance peace in the world. Here, the "unity" discovered in dialogue becomes a foundation for peacebuilding. In his words, "Wherever and whenever men and women are enlightened by the splendor of truth, they naturally set out on the path of peace. . . . Therefore, interreligious dialogue provides a valuable contribution to building peace on a solid foundation."[1]

Pope Francis's Dialogue of Fraternity

Pope Francis developed what he calls the "Dialogue of Fraternity." Its goal is to create a foundational and unifying interreligious brotherhood and sisterhood, the original meaning of the word "fraternity" in the Christian tradition. On this foundation, persons of different religions can jointly address the social and environmental ills at the local level of engagement. In the words of Pope Francis:

> Each one of us is called to be an artisan of peace, by uniting and not dividing, by extinguishing hatred and not holding on to it, by opening paths to dialogue and not by constructing new walls! Let us dialogue and meet

---

[1] Presentation in Washington, DC, on April 17, 2008.

each other in order to establish a culture of dialogue in the world, a culture of encounter![2]

The 2014 Vesakh Message to all Buddhists from Cardinal Jean-Louis Tauran, then president of the Pontifical Council for Interreligious Dialogue, states that Pope Francis is calling us:

> To cooperation with other pilgrims and with people of good will to respect and defend our shared humanity ... drawing upon our different religious convictions ... to be *outspoken* in denouncing all those social ills which damage fraternity, to be *healers* who enable others to grow in selfless generosity, and to be *reconcilers* who break down the walls of division and foster genuine brotherhood between individuals and groups in society. . . . Our world today is witnessing a growing sense of our common humanity and a global quest for a more just, peaceful, and fraternal world. . . .
>
> Dear Friends, to build a world of fraternity, it is vitally important that we join forces to educate people, particularly the young, to seek fraternity, to live in fraternity, and to dare to build fraternity. We pray that your celebration

---

[2] Address, September 30, 2013.

of Vesakh will be an occasion to rediscover and promote fraternity anew, especially in our divided societies.³

Cardinal Tauran emphasizes Pope Francis's call for a dialogue that meets the need to develop a sense of "fraternity" as a foundation for the fourth type of dialogue. The dialogue of action needs to address the social ills of our world. True solidarity in such action must be based on fraternity at the local level.

The Vatican's First Dialogue of Fraternity: Bodh Gaya, India

The PCID began this new dialogue of fraternity with Buddhists at Bodh Gaya, India—the place of the Buddha's enlightenment—February 12 and 13, 2015. Sixty Buddhist and Catholic leaders from eight countries in South and Southeast Asia attended. The topic of the dialogue was "Family: The Basic Cell of Society and Global Solidarity between Religions." The dialogue was led by Archbishop Felix Machado, president of the Office of Ecumenical and Interreligious Affairs for the Federation of Asian Bishops' Conferences (FABC), and the Office for Interreligious Dialogue of the Catholic Bishops' Conference of India (CBCI). The dialogue focused on how to collaborate to build strong families and protect children from human trafficking and abuse. These are specific social ills at the local level in that region of the world. The participants discussed the following topics:

- "We belong to One Human Family"

---

3 On the Vesakh Buddhist celebration each year for the past twenty-five years, the PCID has sent to Buddhists around the world a personal message of unity.

- "From a Culture of Diversity to a Culture of Solidarity"

- "Fraternity, a Prerequisite for Overcoming Social Evils"

- "Fraternity Wipes Away Tears"

- "Together Fostering Fraternity: The Way Forward"

This is an example of how the Pope's new "dialogue of fraternity" seeks a fraternal foundation to reach a higher level of relational engagement in order to address social ills. The discussions focused on strengthening family life, providing values education to adults and youth, and addressing the evils of human trafficking. The Catholic and Buddhist participants agreed that upon return to their home cities, they would work together to pursue the following goals in the spirit of fraternity:

- Strengthen interfaith connections between families, adults and children in communities, neighborhoods, educational institutions, and places of worship.

- Build programs of interreligious awareness and peacebuilding for children, youth, and families in educational institutions and workplaces.

- Forgive and forget the past negative history of conflict and violence and move forward to build peace-loving people in solidarity.

- Train younger generations in joint formation centers to overcome prejudice, study other religions, and build solidarity to protect one another against social evils like human trafficking.

- Build interreligious fraternity as brothers and sisters supporting and revitalizing family life in order to make society prosper.

The Vatican's Second Dialogue of Fraternity: Castel Gandolfo, Italy

From June 23 to 27, 2015, a "Buddhist-Catholic Dialogue on Suffering, Liberation, and Fraternity" was held at the Mariapolis Center in Castel Gandolfo, Italy, sponsored by the Bishops' Committee for Ecumenical and Interreligious Dialogue (BCEIA) of the United States Conference of Catholic Bishops (USCCB) in collaboration with the PCID. This second dialogue of fraternity included forty-five Buddhist and Catholic participants from New York City, Washington, DC, Chicago, Los Angeles, and San Francisco. The United States was chosen for this encounter since it has many Buddhists from different traditions. I was asked to organize the conference by choosing the participants, determining the site, and planning the program.

Presentations on the first day of the dialogue addressed the theme: "Relational Suffering and its Causes." These presentations nourished our common compassion for those who are suffering due to relationships between persons and between persons and the environment. The following formal presentations were delivered:

- "The Causes of Relational Suffering and their Cessation According to Theravada Buddhism"

- "Suffering and the Teachings of Jesus Christ"

- "The Teachings of the Buddha that Posit Relations as Sacred"

- "The Understanding of Suffering in the Early Christian Church"

- "Relational Suffering: Causes and Liberation According to Mahayana Buddhism"

- "Causes of Relational Suffering between Persons According to the Tradition of the Church Mothers"

The second day was spent addressing the ways in which Buddhism and Christianity have sought to liberate persons and the environment from relational suffering. The latter topic was timely since Pope Francis had just published his encyclical on the environment, *Laudato Si'*. Formal presentations the second day included the following:

- "Mahayana Practices for Healing, Reconciliation, and Peace"

- "To Bind, to Heal, to Reconcile: The Church and Interreligious Dialogue"

- "A Buddhist Ethical Approach to Healing, Reconciliation, and Peace"

- "Catholic Theology of Creation: Nature's Value and Relation to Humankind"

- "The Buddha Was Enlightened Under a Tree: A Buddhist Perspective on Nature and the Climate Crisis"

The third day was devoted to a discussion of how fraternal relations as brothers and sisters can be the way forward in addressing relational suffering today. Here, we explored how the love and compassion we had discussed can be lived in fraternal relations:

- "The Four Divine Abodes and Fraternity: A Theravada Perspective"

- "Fraternity in the Christian Tradition: *Koinonia* as an Interpretive Hermeneutic"

- "The Great Compassion and Fraternity in Mahayana Buddhist Traditions"

- "Fraternity in the Catholic Monastic Tradition"

- "Fraternity as the Way Forward: the Religions for Peace Perspective"

- "Building a Fraternal World: A Won Buddhist Perspective"

- "Survey of Catholic Social Teachings"

On the fourth day, we discussed social ills in the United States looked at from various Buddhist and Catholic viewpoints:

- "Social Ills and Possible Social Action in the United States: The Need to Support Families and Youth"

- "Partnerships in Social Services and Dialogue: Lessons from Manhattan, Staten Island, and the Bronx"

- "A Catholic View of Social Concerns in the United States"

- "Buddhist Views of Social Concerns in the United States"

- "Catholic Thoughts on Collaboration in Addressing Social Ills in the United States"

- "Buddhist Thoughts on Collaboration in Addressing Social Ills in the United States"

- "On the Practical Applications of Catholic Social Teaching"

- "Understanding Power, Privilege, Intent, and Impact in Catholic-Buddhist and Buddhist-Catholic Social Change Initiatives"

Finally, the dialogue was concluded with drafting the following list of possible Buddhist-Catholic dialogues of fraternity that address social and environmental ills in our cities:

- Creating outreach programs for youth

- Collaborating in prison/jail ministries and restorative justice matters

- Developing resources for the homeless such as affordable housing

- Educating and providing resources to address the issue of immigration

- Collaborating to create projects with local Catholic parishes and Buddhist communities to address neighborhood social issues

- Developing social outreach programs for value education to families

In closing, Cardinal Tauran told us that Pope Francis had invited us to a private audience. I was impressed that Pope

Francis also requested that we bring the housekeeping staff because otherwise, they would never have a chance to shake his hand. At the audience, Pope Francis shook hands and talked to each of us. When he came to me, I asked him for a blessing. He took my hands and looked down and prayed for me. Then, he looked in my eyes for a moment and put his head down to pray again for me. When he had finished greeting us, he stood in the middle of our half circle and said:

> Good morning. I thank you for this visit, which I have so close to my heart. It is a visit of fraternity, of dialogue, and of friendship, and this is a good thing. This is healthy. In this moment in history, so wounded by wars and by hate, these small gestures are seeds of peace and fraternity. You will plant seeds of peace together. And they will grow into something large. I thank you very much and wish that the Lord bless you.

Looking back at this dialogue of fraternity, the atmosphere was very different from past dialogues of the PCID. Each morning, we would all sit in a room for meditation led each day by a different Buddhist elder. Then, we would walk down the hall to the chapel for Mass. Each day, there would be a different type of Mass: a typical parish Mass, a Benedictine Mass, an Eastern Orthodox Mass, and a Latin Mass. The Buddhists were quite interested in the different ways the priests sang the liturgy. There was also a sense of brotherhood and sisterhood at the meals that were especially prepared for the Buddhists and held at a time that the Theravada monastics could follow their discipline by having their daily meal before noon.

I found that the Buddhists responded to the dialogue's call for us to be brothers and sisters. The Japanese Buddhists included Reverend Patti Nakai, Reverend Ron Miyamura, Bishop Noriaki Ito, and Reverend Ronald Kobata—all Pure Land Buddhists with devotion to Amida Buddha. I felt deeply at home with them. Indeed, I was later invited to give a talk about the dialogue at their convention in Los Angeles. I was the only non-Japanese in a group of 500 Japanese Americans. At meals, they would talk to me about their experience during World War II of being sent to intern camps in the desert. They said that it was even more difficult returning home and finding that non-Japanese persons had taken their property. Also, no one would give them a job. They eventually just worked in the fields. I was touched that they shared this painful part of American history with me.

There were two Won Buddhists from Korea: Reverend Sangwon Hwang and Reverend Chung Ohun Lee, both at temples in the United States. We enjoyed sitting at a café on the square in front of the Pope's summer palace and talking like brothers and sisters. Our friendship has continued to this day. As I wrote above, the Focolare and the Rissho Kosei-kai from Japan have close ties. I spent time with Reverend Kyoichi Sugino from the Religions for Peace at the UN. He always referred to me as his "big brother" since we were now brothers in the spirit of fraternity. I met him later at the memorial for 9/11 where Pope Francis commemorated that terrible day. We walked arm in arm in silence.

I felt close to three other Buddhists, Bhante Chao Chu from Sri Lanka, Venerable Abbot Thich Tu-Luc from Vietnam, and Dr. Sovan Tun from Cambodia, who all live in the United States. Bhante was with me at the national gathering of Thai Buddhist monks a year later where I spoke about our dialogue of fraternity. I respected how they were working with youth in their communities to keep them from joining gangs. Venerable Thich Tu-Luc returned home and joined with deacons at Catholic Churches near his temple, and their youth did service projects for the poor and homeless together as "brothers and sisters."

I have to say that I was not only close to, but very impressed with Venerable Fa Yao, also known as Sak Dhammadipa. He is one of the great scholars in the Buddhist world, and we enjoyed talking about Buddhist philosophy and scriptures. He said to me that he thought that Pope Francis is a Buddha: "When I listen to him, I hear a Buddhist speaking." He was really taken by the Mass. In fact, he said that he felt a divine presence at the Mass: "When I go to Mass, I experience 'something more' than I do when I meditate." He came to believe in the presence of the divine in the Eucharist and would always sit in front of the tabernacle. To this day, he goes to Mass wherever he is. He and his fellow monk—the tallest Chinese monk in the world according to himself—stayed with Ann and me when he spoke at the Buddhist Society at Purdue. We have a deep unity of heart.

Finally, there were nuns from the new Buddhist movements in Taiwan: Venerable Man Pou and Venerable Miao Hsio of Fo Guang Shan, and Venerable Guo Jiann and Venerable Chang Hwa of Dharma Drum Mountain. I have been to both of their monasteries and met their leaders. So, we felt very comfortable with each other. But more than comfort, we shared that we now saw ourselves as brothers and sisters. I later visited one of their temples in New York City with my granddaughter. They loved her and said that she is an "old soul." That was enough for me to respect their deep level of insight.

I also found it inspiring that during the talks about human suffering, we were very much in agreement. And while there were some differences in our approaches to healing, they were very similar. For the Buddhists, the focus is to look within through different practices to find an inner place of peace, loving-kindness, and compassion. For the Christians, the focus is the reorienting of oneself through the grace of God in Jesus Christ deep within oneself. In both cases, the elements of fear, desire, ignorance, selfishness, and hatred need to be overcome, and the virtues of love, generosity, sympathy, compassion, kindness, and forgiveness are of central importance in healing. Going inside, facing one's demons, and finding a deeper peace bring self-acceptance and care for others. In his opening remarks, Cardinal Tauran, president of the PCID, said:

> We are all pilgrims, and I see this Buddhist-Catholic dialogue as a part of our ongoing quest to grasp the mystery of our lives and the ultimate Truth. According to a saying from the Desert Fathers, a brother went to see Abba Moses and begged him for a word. The old man said, "Go and sit in your cell, and your cell will teach you everything." The cell is a metaphor for the inner cell of the human heart where one discovers the mystery of oneself and of God or the Dharma. Another Desert Father, Antony, compares the cell to water, which sustains the life of fish. Without water, fish could die physically; without the cell, a monk could die spiritually.
>
> I see our dialogue of fraternity as an inner journey together as brothers and sisters to address how humanity

has lost touch with this inner cell in his or her heart, and an outer journey to seek together how to share with the poor and suffering of the world a healing balm for our social ills.

The theme for this Catholic-Buddhist dialogue, "Suffering, Liberation, and Fraternity," was based on the Message of Pope Francis for the World Day of Peace 2014 entitled "Fraternity: The Foundation and Pathway to Peace." Pope Francis states that "fraternity is an essential human quality, for we are all relational beings. A lively awareness of our relatedness helps us to look upon and treat each person as a true sister or brother; without fraternity, it is impossible to build a just society and a solid and lasting peace." I stated in my Vesakh Message 2014 that "we live in a world all too often torn apart by oppression, selfishness, tribalism, ethnic rivalry, violence, and religious fundamentalism, a world where the 'other' is treated as an inferior, a nonperson, or someone to be feared and eliminated if possible."

I would like to quote again my words in the Vesakh Message 2014 that invited us all to transform the self-centered humankind in order to build a world of fraternity: "Drawing upon our different religious convictions, we are called especially to be *outspoken* in denouncing all those social ills which damage fraternity, to be *healers* who enable others to grow in selfless generosity, and to be *reconcilers* who break down the walls of division and foster genuine brotherhood between individuals and groups in society."

After discussing the topics of "Suffering, Liberation, and Fraternity" from Buddhist and Christians perspectives, you will spend the last day of the program contemplating and considering how to be *outspoken, healers,* and rec*oncilers,* reaching out together to those in need in your cities. In the midst of challenges, I am sure that the interfaith cooperation based on our shared values can resolve issues of common concern and pave the way for genuine fraternity. For this collaboration, you can count on my solidarity and prayers.

As we will see later in this chapter, what Pope Francis and Cardinal Tauran were calling us to do has now begun.

The Vatican's Third Dialogue of Fraternity: Fulong, Taiwan

The third dialogue of fraternity was held at the Conference Center of the Ling Jiou Mountain Wusheng Monastery at Fulong, Taiwan, in November 2017. The topic was "Buddhists and Christians Walking Together on the Path of Nonviolence." The story about Ling Jiou Mountain is quite interesting. Its Dharma Master, Hsin Tao, traveled as a young man from his home in Myanmar to Taiwan. There, he became a monk at Fo Guang Shan. At one point, he left the order and traveled to Ling Jiou Mountain, where he spent three years fasting and meditating in a cave on the side of the mountain. He did not eat anything besides herbs for nutrition. After he emerged from the cave, he became a famous Dharma Master, founding the Ling Jiou Monastery on the mountain. Today, he has many followers as well as monastics undergoing training. He also has funded education programs and housing for youth in Myanmar.

We visited the Monastery on the mountain and practiced meditation. The Monastery with its mediation hall was built in an ancient Buddhist style. They did not remove any rocks or trees when they built the monastery. So, one might find one or more large rocks protruding from below the floor in the middle of a room. There is a trail up the mountain to the cave in which Dharma Master Hsin Tao lived for three years. The trail swerves in places, so they did not have to cut down any trees or destroy rock formations. At the dialogue, Dharma Master Hsin Tao and I became friends. There seemed to be an immediate link between us. At one point, he said to me, "I think we were friends in a previous life." Be that as it may, I did feel, and still do, his presence in my heart. When we were together, we smiled and laughed and held each other's arms.

The program began with talks on the topic of why we have so much violence in our world. Ven. Chin Shun Wu spoke about how poverty, unemployment, and social inequality, as well as racial and ethnic prejudice, create an environment where violence develops. The dominate class uses violence against the lower class, and the lower class erupts in violence given their situation. Fr. Indunil Kodithuwakku, Undersecretary at the PCID, talked about how religions contribute to violence. He noted that fundamentalism defines persons of other faiths, or of no faith, as enemies of the truth in ways that must be eliminated or controlled. While interreligious dialogue and cooperation can build bridges of mutual understanding in ways that foster peace, fundamentalists are opposed to such action out of prejudice and fear. Kosho Niwano, president designate of Rissho Kosei-kai, gave the following very moving talk about social and domestic violence:

> As a mother of four children, the question of the relation of domestic violence and social violence is very important to me. Buddhism teaches that everything exists in a state of mutual dependence. The family is connected to the community, the nation, and the world. While violence in the home impacts violence outside the home, violence (physical, verbal, emotional, etc.) by leaders of countries affect children . . . they feel insecure or they feel that they can be violent too as they see others doing or saying violent things. Our leaders, especially our political leaders that the citizens look up to, need to be non-violent in

action, demeanor, speech, etc. Also, religious leaders need to stress the true virtues in the family, city, and state. If this is not done, we see bullying and hurtful discrimination leading to violent action. Buddhists teach their children that "all life is equally worthy of respect." There should be no discrimination on the basis of race, gender, ethnicity, etc. With this basis, true religious character development according to Buddhism should include wisdom, compassion, consideration for all living beings, and being attentive to the needs of others. The goal is to live for others, find beauty in what is truly beautiful, feel pain when you see something painful, feel joy when you see others being happy. This is to refine one's sensitivity to other people as well as to all living beings.

The next day was dedicated to "Buddhist and Christian views about nonviolence." Fr. Franco Sottocornola, F.X., quoted a number of teachings of Jesus Christ on nonviolence: "Love your neighbor as yourself" (Mk 12:31). "If you are angry with your brother or sister, you will be liable to judgment" (Mt 5:22). "Do not resist an evildoer. But if anyone strikes you on the right cheek, turn the other also" (Mt. 5:39). Rey-Sheng spoke about the teachings of the Buddha on non-violence. The primary principle is *ahimsa* (nonviolence), which is the first of the Five Precepts of the Buddha. In the early texts, *ahimsa* is an overriding principle. Also, since rulers can build armies, the texts say that the ideal ruler is a pacifist. Archbishop Felix Machado gave a presentation about how today's aggressive and competitive Christian missions are causing challenges to intra-Christian and interreligious harmony in Asia. Venerable Uduhawara Sumanarathana presented the common problem for peace in Asia today: Ethno-Religious Nationalism.

On the third day, the theme was "Fostering Nonviolent Lifestyles." As in the first dialogue of fraternity in Bodh Gaya, the Buddhists and Catholics agreed on the need for education in the family. Venerable Der-Chyuan Lee spoke about the importance of the role of parents and elders in Buddhist character formation. Fr. James Fredericks spoke about forms of Catholic education for Non-Violence. I presented about how fundamentalism, both Buddhist and Christian, has led to violent movements in the East and the West. Finally, Ruei Siang Wu spoke about the new forms of Humanistic Buddhism that focus on compassionate forms of relief services that seek to foster peaceful hearts and minds.

That afternoon, we heard stories about how Buddhists and Christians who teach nonviolence had transformed people's lives. The stories were about Thomas Merton, Thich Nhat Hanh, Albert Poulet-Mathis, Reverend Dr. Martin Luther King, Jr., and B.R. Ambedkar. The rest of the session was dedicated to extraordinary first-hand stories of efforts to build cultures of nonviolence by Buddhists and Catholics from Cambodia, Thailand, Vietnam, Japan, Taiwan, Sri Lanka, India, Mongolia, Hong Kong, Myanmar, and the Philippines.

Finally, the discussion turned to how the dialogue of fraternity developing in Asia can support nonviolence in the future. In this discussion, I realized that the speakers were in pairs from the same cities in each country. The speakers were long-time friends who have been deeply involved in dialogue. For example, from Mongolia there was Fr. Giorgio Marengo and Ven. Kh. Baasansuren. The latter is known as the "singing monk." He sing's popular Mongolian songs as he taps his feet. This is unorthodox for a Buddhist monk, but the Mongolians love him. This national attention has called public attention to the dialogues he has with Fr. Giorgio and his very small Catholic flock on the plains of Mongolia. They planned to create a new dialogue on non-violence when they returned home. All of the other pairs planned to do the same in their countries. They would identify what needs to be done to nurture non-violence and gather Buddhists and Catholics to work together as brothers and sisters to reduce violence in their communities, the goal of Pope Francis's dialogue of fraternity.

Dialogue of Fraternity in Action in the United States

We were all very moved by the words of Pope Francis and Cardinal Tauran at the end of the Vatican's second dialogue with participants from the United States. Both of them gave us a task for when we returned home. In fact, different participants began collaborating in their cities right away. In Los Angeles, Buddhist leaders announced that as a result of the dialogue of fraternity in Rome, their Buddhist communities would join Catholics in immigration reform efforts. In the San Francisco area, monks and nuns of the Vietnamese Buddhist Compassion Mediation Center and deacons of St. John's Catholic Church began feeding the homeless. In Chicago, Buddhists and Catholics began to develop projects that addressed violence in the city by bringing leaders from different neighborhoods together for dialogue.

At the same time, I worked with the dialogue of fraternity groups around the country to see what kind of more permanent project they wanted to do. By the end of 2016, our dialogue groups in three cities, Los Angeles, Chicago, and Brooklyn, brought together two goals from the list we composed in Rome, namely, to build green affordable housing.

Brooklyn's Green Affordable Housing for the Homeless and Elderly

Catholic charities in Brooklyn had affordable housing for families in an apartment complex named Our Lady of Loreto Housing. Our Buddhist-Catholic dialogue of fraternity group along with Catholic charities decided to work together to add a very large building to Our Lady of Loreto that would be for the elderly, poor, and homeless. As of this writing, we have already broken ground for what is called Our Lady of Loreto Phase II. Many elderly persons and couples in Brooklyn can no longer afford their rent. They are forced to live on the streets, in homeless shelters, or in friends' basements. The new phase would provide one hundred thirty-six apartments for poor elderly couples and individuals, and fifty-four apartments for elderly (over sixty-two) living in shelters. The remaining eighty-one apartments would be for homeless persons and couples (over fifty-five) who are frail or disabled.

Due to our Buddhist-Catholic dialogue of fraternity project, Catholic Charities Neighborhood Services (CCNS) will also provide services for senior residents at the housing project. Plus, our Buddhist brothers and sisters from the Dharma Drum Temple plan to provide services such as Tai Chi, pain relief, mindfulness, and meditation practices for the elderly in a Buddhist center that will be part of the project. Those who live in Our Lady of Loreto will enjoy peaceful and safe lives.

Los Angeles's Green Affordable Housing in Skid Row

Skid Row, as it is called, is a fifty-block area with the highest concentration of homeless persons in the United States. Each night, some are sheltered in supportive housing, but more than 5,000 sleep on the streets. Mercy Housing has purchased an empty building at Sixth Street and San Julian in the middle of Skid Row that will be torn down. The housing to be built on that site will create apartments for homeless persons with special needs. Most homeless in Skid Row need mental illness or drug addiction support. Apartments for couples and women with children are also planned. The project will include ninety-five units. The new building will provide a living environment that is safe, healthy, and meets Enterprise Green Standards.

The non-residential space at street level will be designed and programmed to serve the homeless population in Skid Row as well as the residents. Finally, the building will have a Buddhist meditation hall where those living in the housing as well as homeless from the streets can practice mindfulness and meditation to help them gain self-control, anger management, good judgment, and a sense of their self-worth when they are on the streets. Buddhist partners include Bishop Ito (Japanese: Higashi Honganji), Venerable You Heng (Chinese: Fo Guang Shan), Venerable Guo Jian (Chinese: Dharma Drum Mountain), Iris Wang (Chinese: Chu Chi), Venerable Barua Sumana (Thai: Buddhism), and Bhante Chao Chu (Chinese: Los Angeles Buddhist Temple).

Chicago's Green Affordable Housing for the Homeless

Mercy Housing and Buddhist partners in Chicago decided not to build in a dangerous neighborhood, but to expand an existing building in a modest and convenient neighborhood. In this way, they can bring homeless persons from difficult living situations to a safe environment. Mercy Housing's present apartment building for the homeless is named Belray Apartments. The renovated existing building will have seventy apartments, and the new connected building will add thirty-two apartments for a total of one hundred two living units. The addition will also add common space for the residents and their guests. The renovated building and the addition will meet the Enterprise Green Standards to make the housing healthy, secure, and in a pleasant environment so the residents feel at home.

All of the residents will be single homeless men and single homeless women with or without children. There is a school within walking distance from the Belray site. Mercy Housing will provide expanded services for the residents. They specialize in working with the homeless as they do in Los Angeles. The Buddhists involved include Dharma Drum Mountain (Chinese), which is also participating in Brooklyn, and the Jodo Shinshu's Nigashi Honganji Temple (Japanese). The Buddhists will focus on mindfulness and meditation practices that help focus thinking, develop good decision-making, and control emotions. Since the Japanese Temple is walking distance from the housing, the residents will be invited to the temple for social events and meals. Also, through both the Chinese and Japanese businesses in Chicago, the homeless residents will be offered jobs.

Presenting the Green Affordable Housing Projects to Pope Francis

On September 13, 2018, I was included in a U.S. delegation that went to Rome for an audience with Pope Francis. We shared with him the green affordable housing projects from the three cities. We pointed out that three years before at the Buddhist-Catholic dialogue in Rome, he had asked us to plant seeds to address social ills in our cities. We said that we were inspired by his commitment to helping the poor and conserving the environment.

Bishop Nicholas DiMarzio of Brooklyn, the leader of the delegation, said that this kind of collaboration is something "that can be replicated around the world. In the United States, we demonstrate that we can work together, we can collaborate in the spirit of fraternity to give a model to the rest of the world. This is how religions can work together as brothers and sisters for the benefit of those in need."

We also said that Cardinal Tauran of PCID had planned to present the final proposal to him. However, Cardinal Tauran passed away earlier that year. So, the delegation presented the project to Pope Francis in honor of Cardinal Tauran. At that point, Pope Francis showed us a photo of Cardinal Tauran that he always carried with him. He then thanked us, saying that what we were doing was "very good" and had his blessing.

Final Reflections

Looking back at the decades of the Church's Buddhist-Catholic dialogue, I beleive that it evolved greatly during the early days under Pope John Paul II. These dialogues created a worldwide positive relationship with Buddhist leaders. The goals of mutual understanding and appreciation were reached and remain strong. Scholars continued to develop theological dialogues. Monastics continued to develop spiritual exchanges about their lives and experiences as Buddhists and Catholics. Catholic priests, nuns, and laypeople developed friendships and unity with local Buddhists through the dialogue of life.

These dialogues and relationships laid the ground for Pope Francis's dialogue of fraternity. Pope Francis asked us to take another step together in our dialogues. He called us to become brothers and sisters and to experience a deep fraternal unity and joy in being together in the family of humankind. As brothers and sisters, the new and deeper relationship enables us to dialogue from the heart. At this deep level of relationship, we are being called to live together a dialogue of action for the benefit of our family, which includes all humankind and nature. In this way, we can address the social and environmental ills that do such damage to our human family and our home in nature.

I am reminded of Dr. Martin Luther King's *I Have a Dream* speech that one day we will "transform the jangling discords of our nation into a beautiful symphony of brotherhood [and sisterhood]." In this new dialogue of fraternity, Pope Francis has called us, like Dr. King, to get out of our comfort zones, our homes, offices, churches, and temples in order to enter a new world of fraternity. In this fraternal world, as brothers and sisters, we can address the social and environmental ills of our world.

I have found that many are not comfortable with this calling. I am reminded of Dr. King's words from the Birmingham Jail: "All too many others have been more cautious than courageous and have remained silent behind the anesthetizing security of stained-glass windows." Pope Francis, like Dr. King, is calling us to "compose a symphony" as brothers and sisters for humankind and all creation.

www.ingramcontent.com/pod-product-compliance
Lightning Source LLC
Chambersburg PA
CBHW032253150426
43195CB00008BA/442